What about Steven Anderson?

David Cloud

Published by Way of Life Literature
P.O. Box 610368, Port Huron, MI 48061
866-295-4143 (toll free) • fbns@wayoflife.org
http://www.wayoflife.org

Canada: Bethel Baptist Church,
4212 Campbell St. N., London, Ont. N6P 1A6
519-652-2619

Printed in Canada by
Bethel Baptist Print Ministry

When I visit Israel, I feel as if the whole place is just vibrating, as it were, in anticipation of the fulfillment of prophecy. The stage is set for the final week of Daniel's great prophecy, and this is exactly why Israel is back in the land.

Who says that God is not finished with national Israel? The whole Bible says this. It is taught from Genesis to Revelation. The only way to refute it is to allegorize and spiritualize a vast amount of plain Scripture, which is exactly what Replacement Theology does and which is exactly what we refuse to do. No one is going to rob us of a consistent normal-literal method of interpreting Bible prophecy, because the evidence that this is the proper method of interpretation is overwhelming.

If we use the normal-literal method of interpretation, the whole Bible is found to speak with one thunderous voice about Israel and her future, and a handful of isolated proof texts (selected to support Replacement Theology) cannot change or overthrow this clear teaching.

What about Steven Anderson?
David W. Cloud

Contents

The Fruit of Andersonism

The error that Steven Anderson is spreading via his ministry is no light matter.

It will rob you of the Blessed Hope.

It will take away from you the key to understanding Bible prophecy aright, which is the consistent normal-literal method.

It will carry you into the dark forest of Catholic-Protestant allegorical interpretation.

It will separate you from sound Bible preachers whose supposed error is to be "dispensationalists."

It will unsettle your thinking about prophecy and set you on a path to confusion.

It will yoke you together with, or at least put you into communication with and make you sympathetic toward, heretics and nut cases, including "church fathers," haters of the Rapture, and rabid anti-Jews.

It will carry you into a wilderness of wild-eyed conspiracy theories.

It will cause divisions in churches. Not all division is wrong, of course, as both truth and error can cause division, but we are talking about unholy division caused by error.

Anderson's Influence

For several years, people have asked me to publish a report about Steven Anderson.

I first heard of him a number of years ago when I was informed that I was on his "Repentance Blacklist." This is a list of men who preach that repentance means "repenting of your sins" or "feeling genuine sorrow for your sin" or who believe that salvation is *evidenced by* works or that the saved will continue in faith in Christ. Anderson nonsensically labels all such as "ravening wolves" and "sons of Cain."

I concluded that the man might be an aspiring comedian.

Be that as it will, Anderson's influence has spread quickly. His web site claims that over 13 million mp3s of his sermons have been downloaded and his material has been translated into 115 languages. I don't know if this is true, but that is what is stated. This doesn't include his YouTube videos, which have a lot of views. Many of them have a few thousand views, but several have tens of thousands. And his movies *Marching to Zion* and *After the Tribulation* in various uploaded editions have more than a million views, according to Anderson. We don't know how many copies of the DVDs have been sold.

Anderson, or someone associated with him, recently sent some of his DVDs to many Independent Baptist churches in Australia, perhaps to all of them.

Some Independent Baptist pastors have led their churches into Anderson's heresies. We recently had to remove a church from our directory because of the change in the pastor's doctrine on Israel under Anderson's influence.

I heard from a pastor who was forced to resign after an Anderson follower gained the people's hearts.

Another preacher wrote,

"[Anderson's teaching] seems to be gaining a following among Independent Baptists. A group of several Independent Baptist pastors and churches, especially in the southwest, are leading this theological shift. They are very anti-Dispensationalist and anti-Israel, insisting that Israel as a nation has been completely put away by God and has no future. They interpret Romans 11:26 as referring to the 'true Israel,' the church (which makes no sense in light of the immediate context, as well as all of chaps. 9-11). One of their key passages is Gal. 3, esp. vv. 16, 29. I believe they are reacting to some legitimate issues, such as the false teaching in broader evangelicalism that the Jews worship the same God as us and do not need to be saved; the use of the questionable term 'Shekinah' for God's abiding presence; errors in the 'Scofield' form of Dispensationalism; and a blind support for the nation of Israel. However, they have jumped into a ditch on the other side, twisting Scripture, and yet presenting their ideas in a very persuasive and attractive format. I've both heard and personally seen their teaching causing division in Independent Baptist churches."

Churches have lost members and entire families. Anderson's former pastor, Stephen Nichols, says that more than 900 pastors have contacted him through the years with concerns about the man.

Who Is Steven Anderson?

Steven L. Anderson is an Independent Baptist preacher who has wide influence through his YouTube videos and movies.

As a teenager, he made a profession of faith in Christ at Regent Baptist Church in Orangevale, California. After high school he took a missionary trip to Europe, where he met a girl named Zsuzanna while "soul-winning in the streets of Munich." She "got saved," and soon thereafter she flew to the States and they were married in Reno, Nevada. Anderson attended Hyles Anderson College, but left before graduating. Soon thereafter (2005), though very young and inexperienced, a novice at best, he started Faithful Word Baptist Church in Tempe, Arizona, which advertises itself as an "old-fashioned, independent, fundamental, King James Bible only, soul-winning Baptist church."

Anderson says he has memorized 140 chapters of the Bible, which reminds me that Bible memorization, though a wonderful thing, might not keep you from heresy. I think of Jack Van Impe, who is known as "The Walking Bible" for his vast Bible memorization, yet went off the deep end as an ecumenist, date setter, and promoter of Pope John Paul II. I think of Johnny James, also called "The Walking Bible," but who is steeped in Pentecostal heresies.

There are things about Faithful Word Baptist Church and Anderson's ministry that we could appreciate under different circumstances. The church is apparently conservative in dress, music, and separation from the world. Anderson has a large family, and the emphasis of the church is on ministering to families as families and not segregating the generations. (Typically, though, they run even this issue into the ground by saying that not only do they not operate a nursery, they "hate" church nurseries.)

Anderson is outspoken and bold for what he believes, and this stands out in a generation of wimpy preachers.

We believe in strong preaching in the sense of "reprove, rebuke, exhort" preaching. We believe in Enoch (Jude 14-15) and James (Jas. 4:4-10) type of preaching, but that is not what we sense in Anderson. There is something wrong. Mocking, ridicule, cursing, and railing is not New Testament reproof.

I find that he has a strange spirit--not always, but particularly when he launches into the wilderness of his conspiratorial bents, which is frequently. We don't sense godly humility. Those who disagree with him, even on something like the timing of the Rapture, are "demonic" and "wicked" and "deceived." He constantly engages in *ad hominem* attacks, which is a cheap tactic to discredit one's opponent so as to discount his arguments.

This is evidence of a heretical spirit. The word "heretic" in Titus 3:9-11 refers to a willful choosing of and alignment with error, and it refers, as well, to the schism caused by the error. The "heretic" has a heart problem. There is something wrong with him. The Bible says that "he is subverted, and sinneth, being condemned of himself" (Tit. 3:11). This is why he is to be rejected "after the first and second admonition" (Tit. 3:10).

Here is a compilation of Anderson's rants:
www.youtube.com/watch?v=ttxumEkHnKE

Holocaust Denial

In his YouTube video "The Holocaust Hoax Exposed," Steven Anderson says the Holocaust is a "fantastic story that has no basis in reality" and that it is believed because "most people have just not looked at the details." He says, "There is a mountain of evidence on why this never could have taken place."

He does admit that a lot of Jews died of harsh conditions and a lot were murdered, but he does not believe that the Jews were systematically exterminated by the Nazis in World War II.

> "The fact that people were rounded up and placed in forced labor camps does not mean that they were exterminated and cremated to the tune of six million. ... Honestly, these camps--Auschwitz, Treblinka, and others--were probably forced labor camps, not death camps or execution camps. You see, the Germans wanted the Jews working to fuel their war machine" (Anderson, "The Holocaust Hoax Exposed").

Anderson admits that Hitler hated Jews, but he would have us believe that the Nazi Führer simply wanted them out of Germany. "He offered them incentives to emigrate somewhere else." And that is why he persecuted them, "to make their lives miserable because he wanted them to leave." His "goal was to get them out of Germany."

It makes me wonder why Hitler didn't just transport all of the Jews to the German border before the war and say, "Good bye and good riddance"?

Anderson says it was the Jewish Zionists themselves who invented the "myth of the Holocaust" so that the Jews would go to Palestine to form the nation of Israel. They had to invent this story, because before the war most Jews in Europe weren't interested in going to Palestine.

He says that the Zionists and the Nazis were working together toward a common goal until the start of the war. Then Hitler stopped wanting the Jews to leave, but only because he needed their labor. That's when "he started rounding them up and putting them into these forced labor camps." He didn't want to exterminate them and didn't try to exterminate them. He just wanted them to fuel his war machine.

He says the Zionists used the "myth of the Holocaust" to create the modern nation of Israel.

> "That was the justification for going in and stealing land from the Arabs who lived there, and going in there and killing a bunch of Palestinians and kicking them out and putting them into a giant concentration camp known as Gaza, you know, or the West Bank. So we can see the motive to lie about it ... the modern nation of Israel is completely Satanic and it was something that Rothschild was behind and the nations and the world government, etc., which is all proven in my film *Marching to Zion*" (Anderson, "The Holocaust Hoax Exposed," 31:32f).

Anderson says that there are not "the thousands and thousands of Holocaust survivors" who were eyewitnesses of the Holocaust. He says that there are very few who were eyewitnesses of the cremations and the gas chambers, and that "they were lying; it is that simple."

He says it is not surprising that the Jews would lie about the Holocaust since they are rejecters of Jesus as the Christ.

He says "those pictures of emaciated people and emaciated corpses in mass graves" is not evidence of the Holocaust; it is just evidence that a lot of people starved to death, including a lot of non-Jews.

Anderson is a pretty good manipulator of facts. He isn't a master at it; but he is good enough to deceive a lot of people.

Following are some of the techniques he uses in "The Holocaust Hoax Exposed."

First, he doesn't give clear documentation for his statements. He says, "They say..." and, "They all say..." and, "This is the standard story," but his listeners are not told who says the things that he is refuting and when they said it and where and in what context.

Second, Anderson sets up straw men and then knocks them down with enthusiasm, but in the end, they are only straw men.

Consider this statement:

> "The emaciated corpses don't prove the Holocaust, because the story of the Holocaust is that the Jews were just rounded up and brought straight to a death camp and straight to their death."

I have read probably a hundred books about the Jews in WWII and I have visited major Holocaust museums in the United States, Germany, and Israel, and I have never heard such a "story." The real story is that the Jews were killed by the Nazis in a thousand ways, and the death camps themselves were *also* labor camps where Jews were *both* worked to death and outright murdered. It wasn't either/or; it was all of the above! There were times and places when groups of Jews went straight to their deaths; there were times and places when they didn't. The Holocaust was not limited to poison gas and crematoriums, and it was not limited to death camps.

Third, he uses the bait and switch tactic. For example, he points out alleged problems with the math of how the official number of Jews could have been cremated in certain places and then uses that to discount the entire account of the Holocaust.

Fourth, he produces red herrings to make people think he is proving his point, when in reality he is proving nothing. The artifacts that Anderson produces to support his thesis, such as currency from Auschwitz, do nothing to prove his thesis that the Holocaust didn't happen or even that

Auschwitz wasn't a death camp. They are cheap "red herrings," interesting but meaningless and distracting from the real issue.

Fifth, he uses exceptions to overthrow the rule. For example, he talks about professed Holocaust survivors who were proven to be bogus, such as Herman Rosenblat who appeared on Oprah Winfrey, and would have his listeners believe that this is characteristic of all of them and that all of the Holocaust survivor accounts are what he calls "wild eyed stories."

He says, "There aren't thousands of eyewitnesses to the things we are talking about here. There are a handful of paid liars."

Was There a Jewish Holocaust in World War II?

That there was a massive destruction of Jews that was the product of Hitler's "Final Solution" is a well-documented fact of history. It was not invented by the Jews. It is not a figment of Jewish Kabbalah mysticism.

A total of 70 million people died in that horrible war, but Hitler had no "Final Solution" for the British or the French, not even for the Russians or the Polish (except Jewish Russians and Jewish Poles). The Holocaust was an organized attempt to destroy the Jews as a people from Europe, and had Hitler taken over the world, he would have carried out the plan globally. It is not a myth. It was a massive demonic pogrom.

Holocaust museums worldwide contain more irrefutable evidence that the Holocaust occurred. Consider the Yad Vashem in Jerusalem. (Yad vashem is from the words translated "a place and a name" in Isaiah 56:5, and is a misapplication of the prophecy.) The nine galleries in the main museum are devoted to different chapters of the Holocaust, from the rise of Hitler to his death. There are hundreds of photos and artifacts. Arrests in the middle of the night. Destroyed synagogues. Jews marked with armbands. Jews mocked, beaten, spit on, shot, butchered, poisoned. Heaps of corpses. Pathetic faces peering out of cattle cars. Starved men and women and children. The museum maintains a 200-million-page database. As for 2017, the Shoah Database (shoah is Hebrew for Holocaust) contains the names and biographical details of 4.8 million of the six million Jews that died at the hands of the Nazis, with 50,000 new names collected annually ("A Year at Yad Vashem," virtual tour, Nov. 19, 2017, YouTube). They have hundreds of thousands of photographs and 30,000 other artifacts, including audio, video, and written testimonies.

If Yad Vashem is documenting a lie, it is a mega-whopper!

Thousands upon thousands of surviving Jews stumbled out of Europe after the war and testified that their entire families had been slaughtered. Most of the Jews of Europe were gone.

According to Holocaust deniers, it's all a lie and a massive conspiracy, but it's the Holocaust Denial that is the lie, and that, my friends, is no small matter.

Rejection of Biblical Repentance

In my estimation, this is Anderson's fundamental heresy and fundamental spiritual problem. He is the product of and a proponent of repentant-less quick prayerism. This explains his inability to rightly divide the Scripture and his frightful tendency to twist Scripture. It explains his strange attitude, his rage against his detractors instead of interacting with them with godly humility.

His "Basic Soul-winning Demonstration Video" presents a standard "1-2-3 pray after me" technique. In the video Anderson talks to a man at the door of a home. The man doesn't even invite the preacher in, but in a matter of about eight minutes--eight minutes!--Anderson supposedly presents the gospel, gets him to repeat a sinner's prayer, then promises him "eternal security."

That is Quick Prayerism. It is quick to present the gospel in an extremely shallow manner, quick to get someone to pray a sinner's prayer without being certain of what they understand and what they are really thinking, quick to pronounce them saved, and quick to give them "assurance of salvation" on a mere profession of faith.

Unless someone has grown up with the Bible and already has a background in Bible truth, he would have barely a clue what Anderson was talking about in his eight-minute presentation. Try that with a Buddhist in Thailand or a Hindu in Nepal or even with the typical American today who can't name the first book of the Bible or any of the Gospels and is steeped in humanism and evolution.

One doesn't need a Bible Institute certificate to be saved, but it is impossible to be saved without believing the gospel (Romans 1:16; 1 Corinthians 15:1-4). And to believe the gospel requires understanding the following fundamentals of the gospel: Who is God? Who is Christ? What is sin from a biblical perspective? What is death? What does it mean that

Christ died for my sins? What does it mean that Christ rose from the dead? What does it mean that Christ died and rose from the dead "according to the Scriptures"?

We have over four decades of experience in dealing with souls all over America and in dozens of countries, including nearly 30 years living in South Asia, and I have never met a person who could understand the gospel in a saving manner in eight minutes the first time he ever heard it.

Further, Anderson's "soul winning demonstration" doesn't even hint at the necessity of repentance, because he holds the heresy that repentance and faith are the same, even though the apostle Paul plainly stated that they are two different things.

> "Testifying both to the Jews, and also to the Greeks, repentance toward God, and faith toward our Lord Jesus Christ" (Acts 20:21).

Paul preached repentance *and* faith. When preaching in the great city of Athens, he preached repentance.

> "And the times of this ignorance God winked at; but now commandeth all men every where to repent" (Acts 17:30).

The apostle Paul knows a lot more about soul winning and repentance than Steven Anderson, and the repentance that the apostle Paul preached is described as follows:

> "But shewed first unto them of Damascus, and at Jerusalem, and throughout all the coasts of Judaea, and then to the Gentiles, that they should repent and turn to God, and do works meet for repentance" (Acts 26:20).

Paul's description of repentance almost sounds like a works gospel. Anderson should add the apostle Paul to his blacklist of "heretics who preach repentance." But we know of course that Paul's repentance wasn't a works salvation because Paul emphatically taught that salvation is by grace and is the gift of God, not of works (Ephesians 2:8-10).

20

Paul's repentance is biblical repentance. It is not a works salvation; it is *not* a change of life, which would be reformation. Paul's repentance is a change of mind toward God and God's authority over my life that is so real that it results in a change of life. It is a surrender. Biblical repentance is not a change of life; it is a change of mind *that results in* a change of life, and it *always* results in a change of life.

Paul's repentance is the repentance that we see in the Prodigal Son (Lu. 15:18) and the woman at the well (Jo. 4:39) and the 3,000 on the day of Pentecost (Acts 2:41-42) and the Ethiopian eunuch (Acts 8:36-39) and the Philippian jailer (Acts 16:30-34) and Saul (Acts 19:18-20).

The Lord Jesus Christ commanded that repentance be preached. It is part of the Great Commission message:

> "And said unto them, Thus it is written, and thus it behoved Christ to suffer, and to rise from the dead the third day: AND THAT REPENTANCE AND REMISSION OF SINS SHOULD BE PREACHED in his name among all nations, beginning at Jerusalem" (Luke 24:45-46).

Repentance-less "soul winning" is not biblical soul winning.

Salvation Doesn't Have Evidence

Steven Anderson doesn't believe in looking for evidence of salvation. He believes that eternal security means anyone who has prayed the sinner's prayer is saved forever.

This is what he teaches in his "Basic Soul-winning Demonstration" video.

He says,

> "No matter if you quit church, even if you did something awful like kill somebody or kill yourself, ok, God will not take away your salvation from you"
>
> "Basic Soul-winning Demonstration,"www.youtube.com/watch?v=BXMA4xOS5BY, 8:08f

In his sermon "Eternal Security," Anderson says that if a believer killed a hundred people and then killed himself, he wouldn't lose his salvation.

> hardpreaching.com/072306p.mp3, 18:30f

That isn't the point, biblically. The point is that the Bible plainly states that such a person *never had salvation*. He might have prayed a sinner's prayer; he might have been baptized in a Baptist church; but he was never saved, and the evidence demonstrates it.

In "Historic Fundamentalism?" Anderson speaks from the context of 1 John 4:20 and says that a person who professes Christ is saved even if he doesn't love God and hates the brethren.

> "Is it possible for a person to be saved and not love God? Absolutely, because he says here there could be a Christian, if he doesn't love his brother, if he hates his brother, the Bible says he doesn't love God. But he's still a brother. He's still saved. Do you understand what I'm saying?" (Anderson, "Historic Fundamentalism," youtube.com/watch?v=uD73Mr8X0XY, 1:13f).

As he often does, Anderson turns Scripture on its head in his interpretation of 1 John 4:20. He claims that the word "brother" here must refer to a saved person, and therefore a saved person can fail to love God and can hate his fellow man and yet be saved, *even though the verse itself says this is impossible!*

> "If a man say, I love God, and hateth his brother, he is a liar: for he that loveth not his brother whom he hath seen, how can he love God whom he hath not seen?" (1 John 4:20).

The apostle John taught that a saved person will *not* hate his brother, and if someone is guilty of such a thing, he does *not* love God and is a liar for saying that he does. John taught the same thing in other places in his epistle

> 1 John 2:9 - "He that saith he is in the light, and hateth his brother, is in darkness even until now."

> 1 John 3:10 - "In this the children of God are manifest, and the children of the devil: whosoever doeth not righteousness is not of God, neither he that loveth not his brother."

> 1 John 3:14 - "We know that we have passed from death unto life, because we love the brethren. He that loveth not his brother abideth in death."

> 1 John 3:15 - "Whosoever hateth his brother is a murderer: and ye know that no murderer hath eternal life abiding in him."

The fact that John uses the term "brother" in these verses obviously does not mean that the individual is saved. It cannot possibly mean that, because John plainly says that such an individual has not passed from death unto life, is a child of the devil, and does not have eternal life abiding in him. That certainly means that he is not saved. In Romans 9:3, Paul calls the unbelieving, persecuting Jews "brethren," but that does not mean they were saved.

It is the technique of false teachers to take a word and assign a predefined meaning to it and then use that word to overthrow the plain teaching of a passage or even many passages.

There is not one example in the New Testament of someone who was saved and did not experience a powerful repentance and conversion that dramatically changed his or her life. Not one.

The Bible emphatically and repeatedly and consistently says that salvation has evidence.

Consider some examples:

> "My sheep hear my voice, and I know them, and they follow me: And I give unto them eternal life; and they shall never perish, neither shall any man pluck them out of my hand" (John 10:27-28).

Here we see that a true believer has eternal life, but we also see that a true believer will hear Christ's voice and follow Him. That is evidence of saving faith.

> "He that is of God heareth God's words: ye therefore hear them not, because ye are not of God" (John 8:47).

One of the clearest evidences of salvation is one's attitude toward God's Word.

> "Unto the pure all things are pure: but unto them that are defiled and unbelieving is nothing pure; but even their mind and conscience is defiled. They profess that they know God; but in works they deny him, being abominable, and disobedient, and unto every good work reprobate" (Titus 1:15-16).

Again we see that a profession that one knows God can be denied by one's life.

> "And hereby we do know that we know him, if we keep his commandments. He that saith, I know him, and keepeth not his commandments, is a liar, and the truth is not in him" (1 John 2:3-4).

The apostle John was very strong about evidence of salvation. If an individual professes to know Christ but does not obey God's Word, he is a liar. He is not saved. Obeying God's Word is not the *way* of salvation, but it is the *fruit* and *evidence* of salvation. The works are God's works (Eph. 2:8-10).

> "Beloved, now are we the sons of God, and it doth not yet appear what we shall be: but we know that, when he shall appear, we shall be like him; for we shall see him as he is. And every man that hath this hope in him purifieth himself, even as he is pure" (1 John 3:2-3).

John says that the evidence of genuine saving faith is the purification of the life. This is not the way of salvation; it is the evidence of salvation. Eternal security is a present possession and reality in the saved person's life, but the saved ("the sons of God") purify themselves. That is the evidence of God's saving/sanctifying work in their lives.

Replacement Theology

In his video *Marching to Zion*, Anderson teaches that Israel today, the Israel that returned to the land and established a modern state, is not the Israel of the Bible. Rather, New Testament believers are the "true Israel."

> "It's those of us who believe in Jesus Christ that are Israel. ... We Christians are the true people of God. We are the true Israel. And we are marching to Zion" (Anderson, *Marching to Zion*).

Marching to Zion features interviews with Texe Marrs, who sells millions of copies of his conspiratorial books to gullible people and operates a "Bible Home Church," which is an "internet congregation" that you can join by filling out a simple online form. And don't forget to send him your tithe! He says, "We are pleased and honored to pray for your needs," but good luck on getting this "church" to practice James 5:13-16 at your sick bed. This is a "church" without pastors and deacons, without baptism, without the Lord's Supper, without prayer meetings, and without discipline. It is a "congregation" that never congregates.

Marching to Zion also features interviews with the following Independent Baptist preachers:

> Pastor Donnie Romero, Stedfast Baptist Church, Fort Worth, Texas
>
> Pastor M.J. Filenius, 36th Street Missionary Baptist Church, Phoenix, Arizona
>
> Pastor Matt Furse, Mountainview Baptist Church, Custer, South Dakota

Matt is the author of *Who Is Israel?*, which is basically Anderson's *Marching to Zion* in print form. Pastor Furse is not nearly as bombastic and grating as Anderson. He seems like a Christian gentleman, but he has latched onto the same errors. I believe I have met his father, and it is sad that Matt has descended into this error and that his father, Tom, supports it. They've been hoodwinked, and I pray that they will return to the truth.

> Pastor Roger Jimenez, Verity Baptist Church, Sacramento, California (In June 2016, Jimenez said of the murder of 49 people at a gay nightclub in Orlando, "The tragedy is more of them didn't die. ... I'm kind of upset he didn't finish the job." That's right out of Steven Anderson's playbook.)

A major thesis of *Marching to Zion* is that since the Jews rejected Jesus as the Messiah and have continued in unbelief and disobedience to God and since Judaism today is not based on the Bible but on the Talmud, Israel today is not the true Israel. She has been rejected by God and replaced with the church.

Texe Marrs misinterprets Matthew 21:43 to support this: "Therefore say I unto you, The kingdom of God shall be taken from you, and given to a nation bringing forth the fruits thereof" (*Marching to Zion*).

If this verse were isolated, it could teach that God was finished with Israel and that the church has replaced Israel, but it cannot possibly teach that since Christ Himself said that He is not finished with Israel. He said they would not see Him TILL they repent (Mt. 23:39). For more on this see the chapter "Is God Finished with Israel?"

Steven Anderson says, "So in God's eyes, they are not Jews, they are the synagogue of Satan."

But as we will show in the next chapter, the whole Bible plainly teaches that God is not finished with Israel, and we are referring to the Israel that is the seed of Jacob and has 12 tribes, the Israel that rebelled against God and was scattered among the nations as a judgment, the Israel that is still dwelling in spiritual darkness. That Israel is not saved, but God is not finished with that Israel.

Another thesis of *Marching to Zion* is that modern Israel is the product of a giant Jewish conspiracy funded by the Rothschilds.

Marrs says, "Rothschild helped found Israel and Rothschild has always been the backer of Israel. Whatever Rothschild wants, he gets. It is believed that he is the richest man in the world, and I have little doubt of that. ... In 1947, the U.N. voted on a partitioned Palestine. But Israel became the first state and they have never allowed Palestine to become a state. They have made sure that the United Nations provision has never been put into effect."

I am guessing that Marrs misspoke here, but we would note that Rothschild is not one man; it is a family of bankers, and there was a time when they had great power, but by World War II their heyday was long past.

Anderson says, "It was the spirit of antichrist that brought them back to the Promised Land. It was the United Nations who brought them back to the Promised Land."

Another thesis of *Marching to Zion* is that C.I. Scofield was the tool of Jewish Zionists to create a Christian Zionism that would support the modern state of Israel.

This is a conspiracy theory that is strong on innuendo and disjointed facts but lacking *any* solid evidence.

Texe Marrs says, "He [Scofield] had Jewish retainers who had membership in the Lotos club, sort of a secret society. Suddenly he had plenty of money. This corrupt lawyer who had abandoned his wife and was found guilty of numerous offenses as a corrupt attorney. But Scofield was given money and the Oxford group out of England published his Bible. Why would they take a crooked lawyer and make him the editor of a Bible? Then suddenly they have millions of dollars to promote it. With that amount of money, then the Bible took off. It basically sealed the deal for the Jews" (*Marching to Zion*).

Anderson says, "And many evangelical Christians do not get their doctrine on Israel on anything that is written in the

New Testament. They are getting it from the notes of the Scofield Reference Bible. ... So according to the Bible [in Galatians 3:16] the promises made unto Abraham were made unto Abraham and unto Christ and the Bible says in verse 29, 'And if ye be Christ's, then are ye Abraham's seed, and heirs according to the promise.' According to the Bible, we as Christians, whether we be Jew or Gentile, are the heirs of the promises made to Abraham. Those today who are in the Middle East in the nation of Israel they are not in Christ. 99% of them do not believe in the Lord Jesus Christ. Therefore they are not the seed of Abraham. Therefore Genesis 12:1-3 does not apply to them" (*Marching to Zion*).

This is Anderson's standard method of interpretation. I've watched several of his videos but I have yet to hear him interpret Scripture properly when he is trying to prove his pet doctrines. To say that the New Testament believer is Abraham's seed in Christ is not to say that Israel today is not the seed of Abraham. Israel is the seed of Abraham even in her rebellion, and nothing can change that. She is not saved. She isn't in the center of God's will and blessing, but she is the seed of Abraham.

As for Dispensational Theology and its rise in the late 19th and early 20th century, with its enlightening focus on the literal interpretation of prophecy, there is no need to see any sort of human conspiracy at work. Looking at the era biblically, it was a changing of times, and it is God who changes the times and the seasons (Da. 2:21). God told Daniel that his prophecies were to be sealed "to the time of the end" (Da. 12:4). The meaning of his prophecies would not be properly understood until the end times.

I see this as the reason why there was an explosion of literal interpretation of prophecy at the turn of the 20th century, which is the most important thing that Dispensationalism gave to the churches. Israel was beginning to return to the land. The stage was being set for the final chapters in Bible prophecy, and God lifted the veil that had been drawn over the meaning of prophecy by the allegorical Covenant Theology method of interpretation. God opened men's understanding of prophecy in Bible-believing churches.

I recall how as a young Christian I first learned the normal-literal method of interpretation of prophecy and how that it was like a bright light being turned on. I have never accepted all points of Scofield theology, but the normal-literal method of interpretation is a priceless jewel that no one can take from me. When I read the influential older commentators such as the Protestant Matthew Henry and the Baptist John Gill and when I consider their attempt to interpret Bible prophecy, I realize that they were stumbling in the dark in that area because they did not have the key to its interpretation. I get help from these commentaries, but not from their perspective on prophecy.

Our reply to *Marching to Zion*

Anderson and associates talk about the ignorance of Baptist preachers and how they are blind followers, and they claim that this is the reason why dispensationalism is accepted, but I am not ignorant of any of these things and I have not blindly followed any crowd, and I speak for many Baptist preacher friends.

I have studied the Talmud and Kabbalah and world history and Jewish history and American history and Hasidic Judaism and Nachman and the Na Nach movement and Schneerson and the Chabad movement. I have studied all sorts of conspiracy theories. I have studied the history of false Jewish Messiahs. I have been to Mt. Meron and observed the occultic Kabbalah rituals at the tombs of the rabbis. I have seen images of the pagan Zodiac and the Greek sun god on the floors of ancient synagogues in Israel. We have witnessed to atheist Jews and homosexual Jews. We know that Israel is a hotbed of relativistic morality, a mecca for "gays," that the

Israel Defense Force (IDF) is a proving ground for transsexual rights. I know how terribly lost Israel is today.

But neither history nor current events nor Israel's apostasy nor the Bible teach that God is finished with Israel or that Israel today is not Israel or that the church is Israel.

It is true that Judaism is a false religion based on the Talmud and the vast majority of Jews today are not saved and remain under God's judgment that was pronounced by the prophets, beginning with Moses in Deuteronomy 28.

In that one amazing prophecy, Israel's entire history was pre-recorded. God warned that if Israel rejected His Word, He would send great armies that would destroy their walled cities and carry them captive into the nations where they would suffer greatly.

> "The LORD shall bring thee, and thy king which thou shalt set over thee, unto a nation which neither thou nor thy fathers have known; and there shalt thou serve other gods, wood and stone. And thou shalt become an astonishment, a proverb, and a byword, among all nations whither the LORD shall lead thee" (Deuteronomy 28:36-37).

> "And the LORD shall scatter thee among all people, from the one end of the earth even unto the other; and there thou shalt serve other gods, which neither thou nor thy fathers have known, *even* wood and stone. And among these nations shalt thou find no ease, neither shall the sole of thy foot have rest: but the LORD shall give thee there a trembling heart, and failing of eyes, and sorrow of mind: And thy life shall hang in doubt before thee; and thou shalt fear day and night, and shalt have none assurance of thy life: In the morning thou shalt say, Would God it were even! and at even thou shalt say, Would God it were morning! for the fear of thine heart wherewith thou shalt fear, and for the sight of thine eyes which thou shalt see" (Deuteronomy 28:64-67).

The dispersal judgment began to be fulfilled with the Assyrian destruction of the northern kingdom, followed by the Babylonian destruction of Judah and Solomon's temple.

Ever since, Israel has been under the Times of the Gentiles. Though she returned after the 70 Year Captivity and rebuilt the temple, the glory of God has never returned. Ezekiel described the glory of God departing from Solomon's Temple before its destruction (Eze. 9), and nowhere in Scripture do we see that God's glory ever returned. It didn't return to Nehemiah's temple. Israel has been under the control of Persia and Rome and the Crusaders and Muslim caliphates and the Ottomans and Britain, and even today she remains at the beck and call of America and the European Union and the United Nations. She has never repented and gotten right with God. The Talmud is Phariseeism inscribed in books. The Talmud is the very thing that Jesus so sharply reproved in Matthew 23, the very tradition that was behind His rejection and crucifixion. The Kabbalah is blind occultic mysticism.

When we go to Israel, we don't consider the Jews fellow brethren, spiritually. We believe that they are Abraham's seed and God's chosen nation, but they are lost. They need to be saved. We preach the gospel to them. Ask our tour guides! We visit the Western Wall and the tombs of the rabbis, but what we see there is spiritual blindness. Orthodox Jewish tradition is not based on the Bible.

But this does not mean that God is finished with Israel or that Israel today is not Israel or that the church is Israel.

Israel today is indeed rebellious and lost, as Paul said (Romans 10:1), but Israel is still Abraham's seed.

As we will see in the study on the Abrahamic Covenant in the chapter "Is God Finished with Israel?," the covenant promised personal blessings, national blessings, and universal blessings. Paul teaches us that all of the blessings come through Abraham's greater Seed, Christ (Gal. 3:16), but Paul also taught that Israel today is still Abraham's seed, though not yet restored and blessed and not children of God (Ro. 11:1; 2 Co. 11:22).

Israel still is the inheritor of that land; and those who bless her are blessed and those who curse her are cursed. God has used many nations to judge Israel when she sinned, but He always judged those pagan nations afterwards.

Jeremiah 30:16 says "all they that devour thee shall be devoured."

Isaiah 33:1 pronounces woe upon "the spoilers," referring to the spoilers of Israel. God used the spoilers to judge sinning Israel, but He pronounced woe upon the spoilers.

This applied first to Assyria. She was God's instrument to judge Israel, but God said, "Wherefore it shall come to pass, that when the Lord hath performed his whole work upon mount Zion and on Jerusalem, I will punish the fruit of the stout heart of the king of Assyria" (Isa. 10:12). God said that Assyria will be destroyed but Israel will be restored:

> "And it shall come to pass in that day, that the remnant of Israel, and such as are escaped of the house of Jacob, shall no more again stay upon him that smote them; but shall stay upon the LORD, the Holy One of Israel, in truth. The remnant shall return, even the remnant of Jacob, unto the mighty God. For though thy people Israel be as the sand of the sea, yet a remnant of them shall return: the consumption decreed shall overflow with righteousness. ... Therefore thus saith the Lord GOD of hosts, O my people that dwellest in Zion, be not afraid of the Assyrian: he shall smite thee with a rod, and shall lift up his staff against thee, after the manner of Egypt. For yet a very little while, and the indignation shall cease, and mine anger in their destruction. ... And it shall come to pass in that day, that his burden shall be taken away from off thy shoulder, and his yoke from off thy neck, and the yoke shall be destroyed because of the anointing" (Isaiah 10:20-22, 24, 25, 27).

God said the same thing of Babylon. He said that He would take vengeance on Babylon for destroying Israel's temple.

"The voice of them that flee and escape out of the land of Babylon, to declare in Zion the vengeance of the LORD our God, the vengeance of his temple" (Jer. 50:28).

"Make bright the arrows; gather the shields: the LORD hath raised up the spirit of the kings of the Medes: for his device is against Babylon, to destroy it; because it is the vengeance of the LORD, the vengeance of his temple" (Jer. 51:11).

When the remnant of Israel called for vengeance on Babylon, God answered them and promised vengeance:

"The violence done to me and to my flesh be upon Babylon, shall the inhabitant of Zion say; and my blood upon the inhabitants of Chaldea, shall Jerusalem say. Therefore thus saith the LORD; Behold, I will plead thy cause, and take vengeance for thee; and I will dry up her sea, and make her springs dry. And Babylon shall become heaps, a dwellingplace for dragons, an astonishment, and an hissing, without an inhabitant" (Jer. 51:35-37).

In Zechariah 1:15, God said that He was sore displeased with the heathen that destroyed Israel because "they helped forward the affliction."

In Zechariah 2:8-9, God says that Israel is the apple of His eye, and He warns that He will judge those who destroy Israel.

The prophet Ezekiel addressed many nations and pronounced judgment upon them for hating Israel. See Eze. 25:3-7 (Ammonites), Eze. 25:8-11 (Moab), Eze. 25:12-14 (Edom), Eze. 25:15-17 (Philistines), Eze. 26:2-5 (Tyre), Eze. 28:22-24 (Zidon), Eze. 35:3-15 (Edom).

See also Joel 3:19; Amos 1:3, 6, 9, 11, 13; Obadiah 10-16; Zephaniah 2:8-11.

Ezekiel promises that Israel will be regathered, restored, sanctified, and blessed *in the land that God gave to Jacob*, but that God will judge "all those that despise them round about them" (Eze. 28:25-26).

This applies to all of the pagan nations that God has used to chasten Israel, including Rome and those who tormented

Israel during her Diaspora. Ultimately God's woe against the spoilers of Israel will fall on the final pagan kingdom headed by the antichrist.

Israel is under God judgment today for her unbelief, but she is still Israel, and she still belongs to God, and she is still under God's watchcare, and those who curse her are still cursed. I, for one, would not curse Israel, even in her most apostate condition. When Israel was wandering in the wilderness because of her sin and unbelief, God did not allow Balaam to curse her. "How shall I curse, whom God hath not cursed? or how shall I defy, *whom* the LORD hath not defied?" (Nu. 23:8).

I believe we can see this biblical principle at work in the history of Great Britain. After Britain turned against Israel and renounced the Balfour Declaration, which was a solemn promise because of Jewish help during World War I, and Britain did everything she could to arm the Arabs and to disarm the Jews prior to and after 1948, she soon lost her empire.

As for America being blessed or cursed according as she has blessed or cursed Israel, this is not a simple issue to demonstrate one way or the other, since America is a wicked nation in her own right and there are many factors in God's blessing or cursing of a nation. Israel and America today are very similar. Both have had great light yet have brashly rejected the Word of God. Over the past 60 years, America has wielded a great global influence for spiritual and moral *evil*. America has been at the forefront of creating a global pop culture that thumbs its nose at God's holy laws.

By the way, one of the many glaring omissions in Anderson's movies is the blessing that the Jews have been to America.

Jews fought and shed their blood in America's War of Independence and helped finance the war. Humanly speaking, there would not be an America without Jewish money, which is so despised by conspiratoralists. Haym

Salomon was the prime financier of the conflict. He worked closely with Robert Morris, Superintendent of Finance for the Continental Congress. Salomon was twice arrested by the British, and the second time he was sentenced to death, but he was able to escape to Philadelphia. He arranged for the lending of the massive sum of $650,000 (in 18th century currency) to the American cause. When the American army was bankrupt in 1781, Salomon raised $20,000 in loans so that Washington could defeat the British at Yorktown. (To its discredit, the newly liberated colonies did not repay the Salomon loans and he died in poverty before the writing of the Constitution and before the first president, George Washington, nobly led the nation in satisfying all of its wartime creditors.)

Some half a million Jews volunteered for military service in World War II. This represented about half of Jewish males between 18 and 50.

Jews have often been at the forefront of American ingenuity and have won a large percentage of America's Nobel prizes.

Further, though America has been Israel's best friend among the nations, America has been far from a faithful friend. Though President Harry Truman eagerly recognized Israel's statehood in May 1948, the U.S. State Department and the FBI refused to allow any military equipment to be supplied or sold to Israel when she was in a most desperate situation, being attacked by modern, well equipped Arab armies and lacking even basic military equipment such as rifles and bullets and artillery, let alone tanks and planes. The State Department even tried to keep Israel's agents from purchasing the used equipment that was available in massive quantities after World War II. It was sold for scrap, but not to Israelis. Some Americans who tried to assist Israel in the War of Independence lost their citizenship. (This history can be found in many books, such as *The Edge of the Sword: Israel's War of Independence* by Netanel Lorch and *I Am My*

Brother's Keeper: American Volunteers in Israel's War for Independence by Jeffrey and Craig Weiss.)

How does that add up to blessing Israel? And in the Yom Kippur War, when Israel was on the verge of being overrun and destroyed, America did not lift a finger to help until President Nixon was convinced that Israel was going to use the atomic bomb. Only then was Operation Nickel Grass put into place. This massive airlift was the turning point in Israel's war, but it was grudging and almost too late.

It has been observed that America has deteriorated in morality and power and economy and other ways since the modern state of Israel was born in 1948, and this is supposed to prove that America's support for Israel has not resulted in blessing, but I have seen no evidence that the two are connected. Since the middle of the 20th century, America has turned away from God and the Bible in a shocking way, but that is not Israel's fault, and it has nothing to do with America's actions toward the state of Israel. It is the result of America's own rebellion and apostasy. Both nations are rebels against God's Word. Both nations are playing a major role in end-time apostasy, and both are drinking from the waters of end-time apostasy.

A lawyer friend made the following observation:

> "In any event, to be saved from an eternity in hell, one must, no matter his genealogy, repent of his sin and accept the Lord Jesus as Savior, basing it all on His work at the cross and His resurrection. Having said that, it is ridiculous to claim that any particular ethnic group is the 'source' of sin. Gentiles sin like madness itself, with or without Jewish help. Jews sin the same way, with or without Gentile help. It is true that Jews are overrepresented in the pornography industry. But so what? Who's buying the porn? Who supports the industry? And many pornographers (most of the most influential) are not Jewish. Besides, Israel is the human tool used by God to save all of us. The people I identify with historically are largely Jewish (David, Isaiah, Elijah, Josiah, Hezekiah, Peter, Paul, John, etc.). I love Israel,

though I recognize it is in rebellion at this time. I also love the U.S., though I recognize it will be destroyed for its rebellion. The bottom line is that all men are responsible for their own sinning. The heart is deceitful above all things, and desperately wicked. It pants for wickedness like a man dying of thirst pants for water. No ethnic group is particularly responsible or free of responsibility."

Anderson and friends cite a wide variety of Jewish conspiracy theories that propose that the Jews are at the forefront of powerful secret cabals that are the puppet masters behind the New World Order. A great variety of evil is attributed to the Jewish puppet masters. "Zionists" are said to have provoked Hitler into seeking revenge against them. Zionists allegedly planned a "genocide" against Germany. They created the story of the Holocaust in order to create modern Israel. They killed George S. Patton because he knew their plans. They were behind the assassination of American presidents. Zionists invented Islamic terrorism and created ISIS. They supposedly control America and the world's economy.

Consider quotes from Matt Furse's *Who Is Israel?* Furse, who appears in and recommends Anderson's *Marching to Zion*, quotes a wide variety of rabid anti-Jew and anti-Israel publications and wild eyed conspiratorial web sites. Whether or not Pastor Furse himself is "anti-Jew," his Replacement Theology and conspiratorial bent has brought him into association with these people.

> "The power of Israel is staggering. Through recently uncovered documents, it is believed that both JFK and RFK were assassinated as a result of the President and his brother's investigation into certain Zionist special interest groups (such as AIPAC), along with JFK's hard stance on Israel's nuclear weapons, and also for President Kennedy's desire to print American money--without the aid of the Jewish-controlled Federal Reserve" (*Who Is Israel?*, Kindle Loc. 1821).

"Patton knew that the policies for the genocide and destruction of the German people originated from the Jews in Washington DC surrounding Morgenthau and Roosevelt (*Who Is Israel?*, Loc. 1786).

"Benjamin Netanyahu (speaking candidly in a private meeting in the settlement of Ofra, back in 2001, unaware that he was being video recorded) ... 'I want to tell you something very clear. Don't worry about American pressure on Israel. We, the Jewish people, control America, and the Americans know it'" (*Who Is Israel?*, Loc. 1794).

"... for several years leading up to September 11, 2001, almost all of American communications were/are handled by the following companies--Amdocs, Comverse Infosys, Odigo, and Checkpoint Systems--and, all four of these companies are owned/operated by Israelis" (*Who Is Israel?*, Loc. 1901).

"Judaism is the most closely organized power on earth. It forms a State whose citizens are unconditionally loyal wherever they may be and whether rich or poor. The name which is given to this State, which circulates among all the states, is 'All-Judaan.' The means power of the State of All-Judaan are capital and journalism, or money and propaganda" (*Who Is Israel?*, Loc. 1917).

"Imagine if a 'certain country' wanted to gain political power of motivating its allies into fighting for them, by creating a 'false flag' terrorism? What if they staged acts of 'anti-Semitism' in order to gain sympathy for themselves? What if they were to terrorize their allies using the guise of another group, a group that they themselves are opposed? Wouldn't that be beneficial to their cause?" (*Who Is Israel?*, Loc. 1987).

"It is now widely believed that 'ISIS' had actually originated with Israel and other 'allies' of the West. It has also been documented that ISIS has been funded by Israel and America" (*Who Is Israel?*, Loc. 2029).

"According to General Clark, the fix was in. Israel's enemies were going to be systematically removed, and all under the pretense of a 'war on terror'" (*Who Is Israel?*, Loc. 2046).

"Certainly, not all of the recent terrorist activities have been perpetrated by just random, 'crazy' Islamic people. Some of these acts are way too sophisticated for simple 'radicals.' Someone very diabolically clever wants us (the U.S.) entangled in their web of trying to fight terrorism. There really is a conspiracy" (*Who Is Israel?*, Loc. 2121).

"The Israeli Army is one of the best trained, best equipped, best fed, terrorist organizations in the world ... their entire purpose is terrorism" (*Who Is Israel?*, Loc. 2061).

"It is not Iran who is the aggressor, it is Israel" (*Who Is Israel?*, Loc. 2161).

"The Zionists want to keep Jews in danger around the world, so they oppress the Palestinians to a terrible degree, and make sure that their crimes are done in the name of all Jews around the world, so that Jews everywhere should suffer the consequences, may G-d spare us. And then, when something happens to Jews somewhere in the world, they come out and condemn, when they themselves caused" (*Who Is Israel?*, Loc. 2175).

"The Jews are responsible for Bolshevism in Russia, and Germany too" (*Who Is Israel?*, Loc. 2557).

"The Radical Homosexual Movement is run by Jews" (*Who Is Israel?*, Loc. 3700).

"350 people were arrested and 400 children were freed as Canadian police took down an international pedophile-child porn ring with links to Jewish organized crime mob..." (*Who Is Israel?*, Loc. 3860).

"It is commonly known that the World Banks are predominately (if not all) owned and operated by Jewish families" (*Who Is Israel?*, Loc. 4479).

"Disobedient Jews, charging vast amounts of 'usury', are behind the world's financial problems ... and subsequently, all evil" (*Who Is Israel?*, Loc. 4491).

"Disobedient Jews are part of the reason why we have legalized sodomy and debauchery in our nation ... and, as a result, the subsequent end of our nation" (*Who Is Israel?*, Loc. 4505).

Even if all of this were true (and it's not), a Jewish world conspiracy is a red herring. Israel today is in an apostate, unrighteous condition and has been for more than 2,500 years. This is an irrefutable fact. But even if all of the most fabulous Jewish conspiracy theories were true, it would have no significance in the argument about whether God is finished with Israel or whether the church is Israel.

The Bible teaches us to expect to find today an apostate Israel steeped in sin and idolatry, and that is exactly what we find, but it also tells us *as plainly as it teaches anything,* that God is not finished with Israel and the church is not Israel.

To understand modern Israel, we must turn to the prophecy of Ezekiel 37.

This prophecy teaches that Israel will return from her wanderings among the nations, which is described in terms of a valley of death, in two stages, and in the first stage she will return in a spiritually dead condition (verses 7-10). Verse 8 says, "... lo, the sinews and the flesh came up upon them, and the skin covered them above: BUT THERE WAS NO BREATH IN THEM."

This is exactly *what* Israel is today and *where* Israel is today prophetically. Modern Israel is not a fulfillment of the regathering described in connection with the kingdom prophecies. The land has been developed in an amazing way, but drip irrigation and high-tech desalinization plants are not the fulfillment of prophecies about the desert blossoming as the rose (Isaiah 35:1). Modern Israel is, by her own profession, a secular state and most Jews are secular Jews who aren't religious and don't believe in the God of the Bible. A large percentage are avowed atheists. A minority hold to various branches of "orthodox Judaism," which is a religion that follows Jewish tradition rather than the law of Moses.

Israel's return to the land in such a condition is a fulfillment of Ezekiel 37, but the prophecy doesn't end there.

Israel, the very Israel that has returned in a spiritually dead condition, will be converted and exalted.

Modern Israel is setting the stage for the fulfillment of Daniel's prophecy of the 70 Weeks (Da. 9:24-27).

This great prophecy describes the entirety of God's dealings with Israel from the time of the Babylonian Captivity to the second coming of Christ. The prophecy is specifically said to pertain to Daniel's people, Israel, and it is specifically said to describe the finishing of Israel's transgression, the making of reconciliation for her iniquity, and the bringing in of everlasting righteousness, which will happen at Christ's return (verse 24).

By this prophecy we know that one prophetic week of seven years remains of God's dealing with Israel, and at the beginning of that week the Antichrist will rise and make a seven-year covenant with many in Israel and half way through the seven years, he will break the covenant, desecrate the third temple, and cause the renewed sacrifices to cease, which will initiate the three and a half year Great Tribulation.

Modern Israel is setting the necessary stage for these final events. She is back in her own land. She is preparing for the building of the third temple. She is looking for a peace-making, temple-building Messiah, which is a perfect definition of the Antichrist at the beginning of his reign.

When I visit Israel, I feel as if the whole place is just vibrating, as it were, in anticipation of the fulfillment of prophecy. The stage is set for the final week of Daniel's great prophecy, and this is exactly why Israel is back in the land.

2 Thessalonians 2:6-8 explains why the 70th Week of Daniel's prophecy has not yet been fulfilled, and it has to do with God's great love for sinners.

The one who is withholding the devil's mystery of iniquity program to put the antichrist on the throne of the world is a Person. The withholder is twice called "he" in verse 7. This is none other than the Holy Spirit, who came into the world to empower the saints for world evangelism during the church age as described in Acts 1:8 and who will be "taken out of the way" in the sense of ending His present restraining ministry toward the devil's program. The Holy Spirit is omniscient and has always been in the world and cannot leave the world, but Paul is talking about a particular ministry of the Holy Spirit during the church age. Why is God waiting? Peter explains. "The Lord is not slack concerning his promise, as some men count slackness; but is longsuffering to us-ward, not willing that any should perish, but that all should come to repentance" (2 Peter 3:9).

The Rothschilds did not create the modern state of Israel and could not have created it.

One of the Rothchilds, Edmond James, did fund major projects in Israel until his death in 1934, and the Edmond de Rothchild Foundation has continued funding projects after his death, but no Rothschild could have won Israel's War of Independence or the Six day War or the Yom Kippur War, and I've never seen evidence that they even tried. This is a position typically held by individuals who get their information from myth-filled conspiratorial writings and tidbits of things gathered from here and there on the Internet, and who do not have an extensive enough knowledge of history by which they can weigh the conspiracies.

Israel's War of Independence was against absolutely impossible odds under impossible circumstances.

In May 1948, the Arab League composed of Egypt, Jordan, Syria, Lebanon, and Iraq, a vast, well-equipped modern army, attacked Israel in an attempt to destroy the pathetic little fledgling nation. Ibn Saud, king of Saudi Arabia, said, "There are fifty million Arabs. What does it matter if we lose ten million people to kill all the Jews? The price is worth it" (Howard Blum, *The Brigade: An Epic Story of Vengeance, Salvation, and World War II*, p. 305). Israel was overwhelmingly outnumbered and short of or totally lacking in *everything* necessary to win a modern war. At the beginning of the conflict at the passing of the U.N. resolution in 1947, only one Jewish soldier in three had a rifle of any type. Israel had *no* heavy artillery, *no* tanks, *no* war ships, *no* war planes. America, England, France, Italy, and Russia refused to sell arms to Israel, so Jewish agents spread out across the world in search of any arms they could obtain "by hook or crook." After 18 months of fighting, Israel won the War of Independence against all odds.

Where were the Rothschilds when the fledgling state of Israel had to send out its pathetically few ill-equipped and underfunded agents to try to obtain material? How was their supposed nearly omnipotent power and influence brought to bear in the creation of Israel?

The Rothschilds were and are very wealthy, but the Rothschild world control conspiracy is the mother of all *crackpot* conspiracy theories. I repeat, *crackpot*. It's built on the sand of half-truths and outright lies, but because of the perversity of fallen human nature, there are a lot of people who will eagerly believe an unproven and unprovable conspiracy over the solid truth.

The United Nations did not create the modern state of Israel.

This is another idea that is too ridiculous even to waste time on a serious refutation. Apart from the November 1947 partitioning resolution, the United Nations has done everything it could to harm and even destroy Israel. She is hated by the majority within the United Nations and assisted by only a handful of nations such as America, and even that assistance has often been used as a stick to force her to make unreasonable concessions to her enemies and to give up portions of her land.

It is not Israel that has not allowed the Palestinians to form a nation.

At the announcement of the U.N. partitioning plan in 1947, the Jews were content to settle for that part of the land designated to them, but the Palestinians refused to accept the

45

agreement and went on the warpath to destroy all of the Jews and to take all of the land, as we have seen. Since then, the Palestinians have clearly and persistently expressed their desire that Israel be destroyed and cease to exist. When they are speaking candidly and honestly, they admit that they will accept nothing less. Before the Six-Day War of 1967, Egypt's president Gamal Abdel Nasser said, "Our basic objective will be the destruction of Israel. The Arab people want to fight. We will not accept any ... coexistence with Israel" (Isi Leibler, *The Case For Israel*, p. 60).

Even when Israel has unilaterally surrendered land, the Palestinians have used it as a staging area to attack Israel. For example, between 2005 and 2014, more than 12,000 rockets were fired into Israel from the Gaza Strip.

Israel did not steal the land from the Palestinians.

The land never belonged to the Palestinians. It belongs to Abraham (Ge. 12:7) and Isaac (Ge. 26:1-4) and Jacob or Israel and Israel's seed (Ge. 28:12-15). God told Abraham that his seed that would go into Egypt, which refers to the 12 sons of Israel and their offspring, would be the seed that would inherit the land (Ge. 15:13-21).

Further, the Palestinians never loved and developed the land. It was largely a wilderness before Israel returned. When Samuel Clemens (Mark Twain) visited Palestine in 1867, he described it as follows before the Jews returned en masse:

> "Of all the lands there are for dismal scenery, I think Palestine must be the prince. ... It is a hopeless, dreary, heart-broken land. Palestine sits in sackcloth and ashes. Over it broods the spell of a curse that has withered its fields and fettered its energies. ... Nazareth is forlorn; about that ford of Jordan where the hosts of Israel entered the Promised Land with songs of rejoicing, one finds only a squalid camp of fantastic Bedouins of the desert ... Bethlehem and Bethany, in their poverty and their humiliation, have nothing about them now to remind one that they once knew the high honor of the Saviour's presence ... Renowned Jerusalem

itself, the stateliest name in history, has lost all its ancient grandeur, and is become a pauper village ... The noted Sea of Galilee ... was long ago deserted by the devotees of war and commerce, and its borders are a silent wilderness; Capernaum is a shapeless ruin; Magdala is the home of beggared Arabs ... [The plain of Jezreel is] a desolation ... There is not a solitary village throughout its whole extent-- not for thirty miles in either direction. There are two or three small clusters of Bedouin tents, but not a single permanent habitation. One may ride ten miles, hereabouts, and not see ten human beings" (*The Innocents Abroad*).

It is the Jews who have loved that land and developed that land since returning in the 20th century, and this is because God put that land in their hearts and drew them back to it even in an apostate condition. For 2,000 years the Jews, even in their deepest apostasy, have prayed, "Next year in Jerusalem," because God put that little piece of land in their hearts and they have not been able to escape its draw no matter where they have wandered or how unbelieving they have become.

The fathers of Replacement Theology (e.g., Augustine, Origen) were the fathers of the Catholic Church and were laden down with heresies.

Protestants, such as Luther and Calvin, held to the heresy of Replacement Theology as part of the baggage they brought out of Rome. Those who hold to Replacement Theology are building on a foundation built by theologically unsound men.

We agree that "Christian Zionism" is not Scriptural.

John Hagee is a prime example, and he is the example that is used by Anderson and friends. Hagee says, "I'm not trying to convert the Jewish people to the Christian faith. ... trying to convert Jews is a waste of time. The Jewish person with his roots in Judaism is not going to convert to Christianity" (Houston Chronicle, Apr. 30, 1988).

Another example is Tommy Waller, founder of the Christian Zionist organization Hayovel. He condemns "missionizing" Jews. He calls on "the Christian community to totally and completely replace anti-Semitism and replacement theology with unconditional support for Israel and the Jewish people without trying to change who they are" ("Christian Zionist Leader Calls for End to Missionizing," BreakingIsraelNews, Sep. 25, 2017).

Christian Zionists support the Temple Institute and fund the building of Israel's third temple, though it will not be occupied by Christ but by the Antichrist. They believe in non-critical acceptance of whatever Israel does.

All of that is blatantly unscriptural. We denounce replacement theology in no uncertain terms, but the gospel of Jesus Christ is for both Jew and Gentile. "Neither is there salvation in any other: for there is none other name under heaven given among men, whereby we must be saved" (Acts 4:12).

Instead of some type of "Christian Zionism," Christians should follow the apostle Paul's example toward the Jews in their spiritually blind condition.

He loved them and wanted to see them saved (Ro. 9:1-3; 10:1). He preached the gospel to them "first" (Ro. 1:16). His first stop in any city was the Jewish synagogue. But Paul also spoke plainly about their spiritual condition (1 Th. 2:14-16), and he did not join hands with them in religious endeavors (2 Co. 6:14). The early churches did not invite unsaved Jewish rabbis to speak in their services and thus give them a forum to teach their vain traditions and heresies.

The vast majority of Independent Baptists are not "Christian Zionists." In fact, I don't know of any that are. Independent Baptists follow the example of Paul, knowing that most Jews today are not saved but need to be saved through faith in Jesus Christ, and that Israel as a nation (not every individual Jew) will be saved in God's timing. Every Independent Baptist with whom I have ever discussed the issue of Israel has had Paul's perspective rather than Hagee's or Waller's. Every Independent Baptist mission to the Jews that I have known of has had Paul's perspective.

No one can perfectly reconcile everything Bible prophecy teaches or answer every question that can be asked. No system of interpretation has ever done this. Sincere men on many sides of the issue have been trying to do this for 2,000 years. No "Johnny come lately" is going to come up with new things.

I am nothing special, but am a very serious Bible student, and I have never accepted systematic theologies without testing them by Scripture alone.

Steven Anderson and his disciples claim that the reason that Dispensationalism was widely accepted is that it was not critically examined.

I can't speak for other men, but I have not accepted Dispensationalism or any other theology without critical testing, and I have a few credentials. Not a lot of men have published Bible encyclopedias and complete Bible college curriculums, as I have done. I know that Anderson will mock me as a proud boaster for saying this and will twist my words out of context, because that is what he does to anyone who challenges them, but the Lord knows my heart. I am not boasting; I am simply stating my credentials to speak on this issue.

My zeal in Bible study and credentials in teaching God's Word doesn't mean that my understanding of prophecy is right, of course, but it does mean that I have looked at the issue diligently and passionately for 44 years. I love Bible prophecy. I have looked at it from all sides.

From the beginning of my Christian life in 1973, I had a godly suspicion of any "theology," referring to theological systems. I wasn't led to Christ by an Independent Baptist, and at the time of my conversion I had never attended an Independent Baptist church. In fact, I don't think I had even heard of an Independent Baptist church. I didn't know where to go to church at first, and I searched for a church with a Bible in hand and an earnest prayer on my lips.

From the beginning, I understood that there were false teachers and that it was possible to be deceived. The kind man who led me to Christ took me into a Christian bookstore to buy me a King James Bible and a Strong's Concordance, and as we were walking through the store he said to me, "See all of these books; you have to be careful about Christian books; the Bible warns of false teachers." He taught me 1 Thessalonians 5:17, Acts 17:11, John 7:17 and John 8:31-32, and it was with that mindset that I started my Christian life. As a young Christian, I wanted teachers and I knew that I needed teachers. I was not a "know it all." I wanted help. But I had no intention of blindly trusting any man. I wanted to prove all things by Scripture. That is why I set out as a new believer to learn the Bible. I knew that I couldn't test things by the Bible until I really knew the Bible, and the better I knew the Bible, the more effectively I could discern truth from error. From the beginning, I devoured the Bible. I have probably *averaged* eight hours a day in Bible study and related studies over nearly a half century. I wore out a Strong's Concordance the very first year, and that year, I made my own topical dictionary by dividing notebooks into subjects and writing down by hand every verse (That was before the era of the personal computer.) I then analyzed the verses on the various topics to see what the whole Bible taught on those subjects. In other words, I started my own systematic theology studies the first year I was saved.

I have owned Scofield Bibles and practically every study Bible that has been published in the past century, but my personal Bible has been a wide margin reference Bible without notes which I have used over the years to make my own study Bible, so to speak. If I remember correctly, I used an Oxford wide margin, then a Cambridge, and after many years transferred the notes to a World Publishing wide margin, which has been rebound.

I have never accepted traditional Dispensational theology blindly, and I don't recommend that anyone do so.

No human theological system is the sole authority. There are things in traditional Dispensationalism with which I don't agree. I have discussed these things with preacher friends. I don't see a clear teaching about seven dispensations in Scripture, for example, and I teach a different way of looking at dispensations in my course *Understanding Bible Prophecy*. I don't think we know how the church and redeemed Israel relate to one another either in the millennial kingdom or in the New Jerusalem. I have unanswered questions about the bride of Christ. The church is referred to as the bride in Ephesians 5, but the bride is also said to be the New Jerusalem that includes redeemed Israel (Re. 21:9-10). What is the relationship between the Jerusalem above and the Jerusalem below? There are many questions to which I have never found satisfying answers. I haven't been satisfied with standard Dispensational answers or with "Progressive Dispensation" answers, and I have been less satisfied with Covenant Theology and Replacement Theology answers, so I keep studying, and I keep learning, and I don't try to understand more than Scripture reveals.

There are problems with every position on the timing of the Rapture.

I know those problems. I have looked at those problems. I have studied what men have written about those problems. I have prayed about those problems. At the end of the day, I find the fewest problems with the Pre-Tribulation Rapture. I find that it is supported by very clear Bible truths. I find that it has an element of simplicity and perspicuity that I believe to be a mark of sound Bible doctrine. (Contrast, for example, Steven Anderson's teaching on Revelation, which is complicated, convoluted, and difficult to follow.) I find *far more* problems with other positions on the timing of the Rapture.

But I am not going to pretend that there aren't any problems with the position I hold today and that I have a doctrine of prophecy that is wrapped up in a nice box with a pretty bow so that I can fully answer every argument that can be made against a Pre-Tribulation Rapture or fully explain every verse of Scripture.

The major points of "dispensational" theology were not first taught 100 years ago; they were first taught 2,000 years ago in the New Testament. What John Darby or C.I. Scofield were, or what the errors of Scofield's theology might be, is irrelevant to *biblical dispensationalism, which predated Darby dispensationalism by 2,000 years.*

I get my theology from Scripture alone, and Scripture teaches me the following:

• The church is not Israel; the church is a mystery not revealed in Old Testament prophecy. It is a parenthesis in prophecy between the first and second comings of Christ during which time Israel is "blinded in part until the fullness of the Gentiles be come in." The church is not seen in the 70 Week prophecy of Daniel 9. It plays no part in Daniels 70 Week prophecy. See Romans 11:25.

• Israel's covenants will yet be fulfilled. Again we cite Romans 11:25-32, which is a key passage on the subject. It teaches the following: (1) Israel is blind in part today. (2) This blindness is not permanent but will last until the fulness of the Gentiles be come in, which refers to the completion of the church. (3) Then all Israel shall be saved. This does not mean that every Jew will be saved, but that Israel will be saved as a whole. The same language is used in Ezekiel 39:25 - "Now will I bring again the captivity of Jacob, and have mercy upon the whole house of Israel." Ezekiel 37:15-28 describes Judah and Ephraim being restored to one nation. The 12 tribes will continue to be the 12 tribes. We see this in Revelation 7. As for individual Jews, we know from other prophetic passages that only 1/3 of the Jews living at that time will be saved (Zec. 13:8-9). (4) Israel's conversion will occur when Christ returns and turns away ungodliness from Jacob. (5) Then the new covenant described in Jeremiah 31-33 and many other prophecies will be fulfilled. (6) Though the Jews are enemies of the gospel today, they are still beloved by God and God's covenants with them are not fulfilled in the church but will be fulfilled literally in a converted Israel.

- The return of Christ is imminent. It is "at hand" (Ro. 13:12; Php. 4:5; 1 Pe. 4:7). This means that the true churches will not see the rise of the Antichrist, for if they see that, they would then know the time of Christ's return exactly because they could count down the prophetic events that are described in passages such as Daniel 9, Matthew 24, and Revelation. If I witnessed the rise of the Antichrist which begins with a seven-year covenant with Israel (Da. 9:28), I would know that the Two Witnesses will prophesy for 3.5 years, then be killed and raised from the dead, then the Antichrist will break his covenant with Israel and desecrate the third temple by proclaiming himself God (Da. 9:28; Mt. 24:15), etc. There would be no need for watching.

- Regardless of the fact that most Jews today don't know what tribe they are of, God knows the 12 tribes of Israel and He will call 12,000 of each tribe at the beginning of Daniel's 70th Week (Revelation 7).

This is *biblical dispensationalism*, because it is based on the teaching of the New Testament itself rather than on any recent theology.

In the next chapter, as a further reply to Anderson's *Marching to Zion*, we will answer the question, "Is God finished with Israel?"

Is God Finished with Israel?

As we have seen, in the video *Marching to Zion* Steven Anderson teaches that Israel today, the Israel that returned to the land in the 20th century and established a modern state, is not the Israel of the Bible. Rather, God is finished with the nation Israel and New Testament believers are the "true Israel."

> "It's those of us who believe in Jesus Christ that are Israel. ... We Christians are the true people of God. We are the true Israel. And we are marching to Zion" (Anderson, *Marching to Zion*).

Other men associated with Anderson are saying the same thing.

> "So I'm Israel. Those people over there are not Israel" (Pastor M.J. Filenius, 36th Street Missionary Baptist Phoenix, Arizona, cited in *Marching to Zion*).

> "There is NOTHING in the New Testament to support the Jewish occupation of Palestine. In fact, Paul clearly tells the believers, that we (saved) are the 'seed of Abraham' and the 'children of promise' (Galatians 3-4; Romans 9)" (Matt Furse, *Who Is Israel?*).

In this chapter we intend to answer this false charge from Scripture.

Who says that God is *not* finished with national Israel? The whole Bible says this. It is taught from Genesis to Revelation. The only way to refute it is to allegorize and spiritualize a vast amount of plain Scripture, which is exactly what Replacement Theology does and which is exactly what we *refuse* to do. No one is going to rob us of a consistent normal-literal method of interpreting Bible prophecy, because the evidence that this is *the* proper method of interpretation is overwhelming.

Normal-Literal Method of Interpretation

A fundamental issue is how to interpret Bible prophecy. If a normal-literal method is used, there can be no doubt that God is not finished with Israel and that the church has not replaced Israel. To say that God is finished with Israel requires an allegorical interpretation of God's covenants with Israel and the Old Testament prophecies about Israel's restoration.

"Normal-literal" refers to the normal way that we interpret human speech. We use figures of speech, such as metaphors, in normal speech, but we understand that these are figures of speech by the context and we know how to interpret them. If someone says, "I'm going out for a run," we know that means that he is literally going to go running. But if someone says, "I'm going to run down to the store," we know that is a figure of speech, and it simply means that he is going to the store.

The same is true for Bible prophecy. It contains figures of speech, but the Bible makes it clear that these are figures of speech and teaches us how to interpret them either by the context itself or by comparing Scripture with Scripture.

I am convinced that Bible prophecy *must* be interpreted by a normal-literal method rather than an allegorical or spiritualizing method.

And if we use the normal-literal method of interpretation, the whole Bible is found to speak with one thunderous voice about Israel and her future, and a handful of isolated proof texts (selected to support Replacement Theology) cannot change or overthrow this vast amount of clear teaching.

Following are some of the reasons why we know that prophecy must be interpreted by the normal-literal method:

1. God gave the Scriptures to REVEAL truth to man, not to hide it. See Deuteronomy 29:29. Prophecy is given to reveal secrets, not hide them. Prophecy is light, not darkness (2 Pe. 1:19). The Bible's final book of prophecy, *Revelation*, is so named because it is given to reveal truth, not hide it.

Prophecy is to be understood in the normal way that human language is understood because it is God's revelation to mankind in human language.

2. The apostles interpreted prophecy literally.

Consider two key passages:

Acts 3:18-21

Peter preached that as there was a literal fulfillment of Christ's first coming to suffer for man's sin, so there will be a literal fulfillment of the prophecies pertaining to Israel's conversion and kingdom.

- The heaven will receive Christ until He returns.

- Then there will be a "restitution of all things, which God hath spoken by the mouth of all his holy prophets." Words could not be plainer. The prophecies of Israel's regathering and conversion and blessing, and the prophecies of Christ sitting on David's throne, will be literally fulfilled.

Romans 11:25-27

Paul also taught that God's covenants with Israel will be literally fulfilled.

- Israel is currently blind, except for those few, like a Peter and a Matthew and a Paul, who are saved.

- Israel will be blind until the fulness of the Gentiles is come in, referring to the church age.

- Then Israel will be saved and her covenants fulfilled. Again, words could not be plainer.

That the apostles and the apostolic churches interpreted prophecy literally is admitted by most church historians.

"The early Church for 300 years looked for the imminent return of our Lord to reign, and they were right" (William Newell, *Revelation*).

Even Augustine, "the father of amillennialism," admitted that there were many in his day [fifth century] who believed in a literal fulfillment of Revelation 20. He said, "I myself, too, once held this opinion. ... They who do believe them are called by the spiritual, Chiliasts, which we may literally reproduce by the name Millenarians" (Augustine, *City of God*, book 20, chapter 7).

The church at Antioch continued to interpret prophecy literally after the allegorical method was invented by heretics such as Origen (185-254). Antioch, of course, was an important church founded by Barnabas and Paul, and it is from this church that the first foreign missionaries were sent out (Acts 11:19-26; 13:1-4; 15:39-41). It was at Antioch that the disciples were first called Christians. Some of the preachers associated with Antioch were Lucian (died 312), Diodorus of Tarsus (d. 390), Chrysostom (d. 407), Theodore (d. 428), and Theodoret (d. 458). These men did not accept the Alexandrian allegorical method of interpretation. They interpreted Bible prophecy literally. Farrar says, "Diodorus of Tarsus' books were devoted to an exposition of Scripture in its literal sense, and he wrote a treatise, now unhappily lost, 'on the difference between allegory and spiritual insight'" (F. W. Farrar, *History of Interpretation*, pp. 213-15).

3. Bible prophecies have always been fulfilled literally.

Prophecies about Israel were fulfilled literally.

Israel's entire history was given in the great prophecy of Deuteronomy 28 (see particularly verses 25, 29, 32, 36-37, 63-67). These prophecies describe Israel's defeat at the hands of foreign powers and her dispersion to the ends of the earth, and they have been fulfilled exactly over the past 2,000 years.

Prophecies of the Nations were fulfilled literally.

TYRE

Consider the prophecy of the ancient city of Tyre in Ezekiel 26:3-16. Tyre was the capital of the great Phoenician Empire. The city consisted of two parts. One part of the city was on the coast and another part was on an island about a half mile off the coast. It was one of the most beautiful cities of ancient times.

- Nebuchadnezzar will besiege and sack Tyre (Eze. 26:7-11). In 573 BC, Nebuchadnezzar conquered Tyre after a

13-year siege. At that time the coastal city was captured, but the city on the island was not touched.

- Many nations will participate in destroying Tyre (Eze. 26:3). Tyre was attacked and overcome by the Assyrians, the Babylonians, the Greeks, the Syrians, the Romans, and the Muslims.

- Tyre's walls and towers will be destroyed (Eze. 26:4). This was done first by Nebuchadnezzar and then by Alexander the Great.

- The city will be made flat like the top of a rock and even the dust will be scraped (Eze. 26:4), and its stones and timbers will be laid in the sea (Eze. 26:12). This was done in 332 BC when Alexander used the material from the ruins of the city on the coast to build a road out to the island.

- Tyre will become a place for the spreading of nets (Eze. 26:5). The great mart of the nations eventually became a lowly fishing village.

- Tyre was a spoil to the nations (Eze. 26:12). After her destruction by Alexander, Tyre did not regain her position as

Siege of Tyre
July, 332 B.C.

the head of an empire; instead, she was the vassal of whatever power happened to dominate the region.

Prophecies of Christ's First Coming were fulfilled literally.

Consider, for example, the prophecy of Christ's first coming in Psalm 22. In this Psalm alone, there are many specific prophecies about Christ's death, and they were literally fulfilled:

Ps. 22:1 – Jesus' words on the cross (Mt. 27:46)

Ps. 22:6-8, 12-13 – The people reviled Jesus (Mt. 27:39-44)

Ps. 22:11 – There were none to help Him (Mk. 14:50; Heb. 1:3)

Ps. 22:14-16 – They crucified Him (Mt. 27:35)

Ps. 22:17a – They did not break his bones (Jn. 19:33)

Ps. 22:17b – They stared at Him (Mt. 27:36)

Ps. 22:18 – They gambled for his garments (Mt. 27:35; Jn. 19:24)

Since Bible prophecy has always been fulfilled literally, there is no reason to believe that future prophecies will be fulfilled any differently.

4. *The Lord Jesus said the major prophetic events are yet future.* In His prophecy in Matthew 24, He described the Great Tribulation and the rule of the Antichrist and said that these events will occur in the future just prior to His literal return (Mt. 24:15-29). It is obvious, then, that the Great Tribulation is not something that has already been fulfilled in history or is being fulfilled, and it is obvious that the Antichrist is a literal man who will desecrate a literal third temple.

5. *Christ rebuked His disciples for not believing the prophecies in their literal interpretation* (Lu. 24:25-27).

6. *The stage is set today for the literal fulfillment of the prophecies.* The machinery for a one-world government and a one-world religion as described in Revelation 13 and 17 is being set up before our eyes. The technology is in place to control world commerce as described in Revelation 13:16-17

and for the people of the world to observe the events described in Revelation 11:8-10. Most importantly, the nation Israel is back in her land in fulfillment of Ezekiel 37:1-14 (which says she will return first in a spiritually-dead condition, verse 8) and in preparation for the literal fulfillment of all her covenants and prophecies. She is making preparations to build the third temple, which will be desecrated by the Antichrist. She is looking for a peace-making, temple-building Messiah, which is exactly what the Antichrist will be at the beginning of his reign when he makes a covenant with Israel. This supports the doctrine that God has not rejected the nation Israel in a permanent sense or replaced Israel with the Church, but has only temporarily set Israel aside until He is ready to fulfill His covenants with her.

7. *Prophecy as an apologetic demands the literal interpretation of prophecy.* In Isaiah, Jehovah God Himself uses Bible prophecy as evidence that He is its Author. See Isaiah 41:22-23; 44:6-7; 45:21-22; 46:9-10. The reason that Bible prophecy can be used as an evidence of the divine inspiration of Scripture is that it is precise and clear. It contains details such as names, dates, and places. For example, Psalm 22 contains the details of Christ's death, including the very words He spoke (Ps. 22:1), the piercing of His hands and feet (Ps. 22:16), mocking crowds (Ps. 22:7-8), the gambling for His garment (Ps. 22:18), and the fact that His bones were not broken (Ps. 22:17). It is impossible for man to know such things about the future. For such details about a man's life to be written in a book hundreds of years before his birth is irrefutable evidence that that book is of God. But if the details of the prophecies are not interpreted literally, the prophecies cannot be used as an apologetic because it will not be clear exactly what is being prophesied. If piercing of the hands and feet, for example, mean something other than a literal piercing then the power of the prophecy as an apologetic is destroyed.

8. *Practical necessity demands the literal interpretation of prophecy.* To interpret Bible prophecy allegorically destroys the absolute sense of God's Word. If prophecy does not mean what it says, there is no way to know what it does mean. Consider Revelation 20:1-3. If this passage does not mean that a literal angel binds a literal devil in a literal bottomless pit for a literal thousand years, we have no way of knowing for sure what it does mean. If it does not mean what it says, it could mean anything that any interpreter says it means.

Consider this important statement by Paul Lee Tan: "Whether it is the interpretation of prophecy or non-prophecy, once literality is sacrificed, it is like starting down an incline. Momentum speedily gathers as one succumbs to the temptation to spiritualize one passage after another. ... Moreover, under the method of spiritualization, there is no way for an interpreter to test the validity of his conclusions, except to compare his works with that of a colleague. Instead of 'a more sure word of prophecy' (2 Pe. 1:19), interpreters end up with an 'unsure' word and chaos in the ranks" (Tan, *The Interpretation of Prophecy*, pp. 73, 74).

J. Vernon McGee was trained in the allegorical method of interpretation, but he realized as a young man that it resulted in foolishness: "I went to a seminary that was amillennial, where they attempted to fit the rest of Revelation into the historical, or the amillennial, viewpoint. It became ridiculous and even comical at times. For example, when we reached the place where Scripture says that Satan was put into the bottomless pit, we were taught that that has already taken place. I asked the professor, 'How do you explain the satanic activity that is taking place today?' He replied, 'Satan is chained, but he has a long chain on him. It is like when you take a cow out into a vacant lot and tether her out on a long rope and let her graze.' That was his explanation! And my comment was, 'Doctor, I think Satan's got a pretty long chain on him then, because he is able to graze all over the world today!' It really makes some Scriptures seem rather ridiculous when you follow the allegorical viewpoint" (*Thru the Bible with J. Vernon McGee*).

We have given eight reasons why Bible prophecy must be interpreted by the normal-literal method, and, to repeat what we said at the beginning of this section, *if we use the normal-literal method, the whole Bible is found to speak with one thunderous voice about Israel and her future, and a handful of isolated proof texts (selected to support Replacement Theology) cannot change or overthrow this vast amount of clear teaching.*

The Abrahamic Covenant

The Abrahamic Covenant says God is not finished with Israel.

God's covenant with Abraham is one of the most important things in human history. By this covenant, God created the nation Israel and brought the Scriptures and the Saviour to the world. By this covenant, God brought salvation to the sinful human race through Christ. By this covenant, God will fulfill His eternal plan to bring together all things in one in Christ (Eph. 1:10).

The Three Blessings

God's covenant with Abraham promises **personal blessings** (for Abraham himself), **national blessings** (for the 12 tribes of Israel), and **universal blessings** (for all of the redeemed)-- not one or the other, but all three.

The **personal** aspect of Abraham's covenant belongs to Abraham himself ("I will bless thee, and make thy name great," Ge. 12:2). Abraham is one of the most important men in human history. He is mentioned 311 times in the Bible. He was blessed by wealth even in his lifetime (Ge. 24:35). Through Isaac, Abraham is the father of the Jews and the Christians, and through Ishmael, he is the father of the Arabs and the Muslims. Paradise is named after him (Lu. 16:22), because he is the father of saving faith (Ro. 4:11; Ga. 3:14).

The **national** aspect of Abraham's covenant belongs to the nation Israel ("I will make of thee a great nation," Ge. 12:2). Israel inherited the covenant through Isaac (Ge. 26:1-4) and Jacob, whose name was changed to Israel. God said to Jacob, "And the land which I gave Abraham and Isaac, to thee I will give it, and to thy seed after thee will I give the land" (Ge. 35:9-12). To national Israel belongs **the land** that was promised to Abraham. Compare Ge. 12:7; 13:14-17; 15:7. In 1 Chronicles 16:13-16 David affirmed that Abraham's covenant passed through Isaac and Jacob to Jacob's children, the nation Israel, and that the promise includes the inheritance of the land.

The **universal** blessings of the Abrahamic Covenant are enjoyed by all believers through Abraham's greater Seed, Jesus Christ ("and in thee shall all families of the earth be blessed," Ge. 12:3). Those who receive Christ become Abraham's seed (Gal. 3:6-9, 29). But New Testament believers do not possess the land of Israel and our hope is not tied to that land. Our hope is not earthly but heavenly. We will rule and reign with Christ, not as Israel, but as Christ's Bride. How exactly the church will relate to Israel in the Millennial kingdom is not revealed in Scripture.

The Seed of Abraham

Abraham was promised a seed. This is mentioned at least 24 times in Genesis (Ge. 12:7; 13:15; 13:16; 15:5, 13, 18; 16:10; 17:7, 8, 9, 10; 17:19; 21:12; 22:17, 18; 24:7; 26:3, 4, 24; 28:4, 13, 14; 32:12; 35:12; 48:4).

There is *national and physical seed.* Abraham's seed is the nation Israel which shall inherit the land (Ge. 15:13-21).

There is *spiritual seed through Christ* (Ga. 3:16, 29). The apostle Paul teaches that all of the blessings of the Abrahamic Covenant come through Abraham's greater Seed, Christ (Gal. 3:16), but Paul also teaches that Israel today is Abraham's seed, though not currently the children of God (Ro. 11:1; 2 Co. 11:22).

The rebellion of Abraham's national seed, Israel, does not annul the promises that God has made to her. Everywhere in Scripture we are taught that national Israel would be judged for her sin, but that she will be restored to her own land and to the place of God's blessing when she repents. In the section on distinguishing Israel from the Church in the previous section on the Interpretation of Prophecy, we looked at many passages that teach this (Deuteronomy 28-30; Hosea 3:4-5; Amos 9:8-15; Acts 3:18-21; 15:13-18; Romans 11:25-29).

Consider Leviticus 26:31-45. This passage describes the judgment that will come upon Israel because of her sin against God, but it says further that Israel will be restored when she repents and acknowledges her sin, and this restoration *is because of the covenant that God made with Abraham, Isaac, and Jacob.*

> "THEN WILL I REMEMBER MY COVENANT WITH JACOB, AND ALSO MY COVENANT WITH ISAAC, AND ALSO MY COVENANT WITH ABRAHAM will I remember; and I WILL REMEMBER THE LAND. The land also shall be left of them, and shall enjoy her sabbaths, while she lieth desolate without them: and they shall accept of the punishment of their iniquity: because, even because they despised my judgments, and because their soul abhorred my statutes. And yet for all that, when they be in the land of their enemies, I WILL NOT CAST THEM AWAY, NEITHER WILL I ABHOR THEM, TO DESTROY THEM UTTERLY, AND TO BREAK MY COVENANT WITH THEM: for I am the LORD their God. But I will for their sakes remember THE COVENANT OF THEIR ANCESTORS, whom I brought forth out of the land of Egypt in the sight of the heathen, that I might be their God: I am the LORD" (Le. 26:42-45).

Words could not be plainer. Israel's rebellion does not annul the covenant that He made with her through Jacob. In this passage, God is talking about the people of Israel and the land of Israel, and there is no legitimate way to apply this to the church.

The Blessing and the Curse

God promised to bless those who bless Abraham and to curse those who curse him (Ge. 12:3).

Laban testified that God blessed him for Jacob's sake (Ge. 30:27).

Potiphar testified that God blessed him for Joseph's sake (Ge. 39:2-3).

The principle of cursing those who curse Abraham and blessing those who bless him is applicable to Abraham's national seed. God has blessed and cursed nations for how they have treated Israel. God has used many nations to judge Israel when she sinned, but He always judged those pagan nations afterwards. Isaiah 33:1 pronounces woe upon "the spoilers," referring to the spoilers of Israel. God used the spoilers to judge sinning Israel, but He pronounced woe upon the spoilers. This happened to Assyria (Isa. 10:25). It happened to Babylon (Jer. 51:11). God took vengeance on Babylon for destroying Israel's temple. In Zechariah 2:8-9, God says that Israel is the apple of His eye, and He warns that He will judge those who destroy Israel. The prophet Ezekiel addressed many nations and pronounced judgment upon them for hating Israel. See Eze. 25:3-7 (Ammonites), Eze. 25:8-11 (Moab), Eze. 25:12-14 (Edom), Eze. 25:15-17 (Philistines), Eze. 26:2-5 (Tyre), Eze. 28:22-24 (Zidon), Eze. 35:3-15 (Edom). Israel is under God judgment today for her unbelief, but she is still Israel, and she still belongs to God, and she is still under God's watchcare, and those who curse her are still cursed. I, for one, would not curse Israel, even in her most apostate condition. When Israel was wandering in the wilderness because of her sin and unbelief, God did not allow Balaam to curse her. "How shall I curse, whom God hath not cursed? or how shall I defy, *whom* the LORD hath not defied?" (Nu. 23:8).

I believe we can see this biblical principle at work in the history of Great Britain. After Britain turned against Israel and renounced the Balfour Declaration, which was a solemn promise because of Jewish help during World War I, and Britain did everything she could to arm the Arabs and to disarm the Jews prior to and after 1948, she soon lost her empire.

The principle of cursing those who curse Abraham and blessing those who bless him is applicable to born-again Christians who are Abraham's seed (Ga. 3:29). God has blessed nations for how they have treated Christians and how they have given liberty for the preaching of the gospel. We can see this today. Those nations that give the most freedom for gospel preaching and church work are the most blessed nations.

The Covenant of Deuteronomy 30

The covenant of Deuteronomy 30 says God is not finished with Israel. It has been called "the Palestinian Covenant," but we believe that a better name is "the Return Covenant." "Palestina" is the name that Rome gave to the land of Israel after the destruction of the Bar Kokhba revolt in AD 135. It is a term that has been popularized by the Muslim Palestinian movement which argues that the land belongs to the "Palestinians" rather than to Israel. The land is not called *Palestine* in Scripture. (The one mention of "Palestine" in the King James Bible in Joel 3:4 is translated from the same Hebrew word as "Philistia" and refers to the coastal area that was occupied by the Philistines.)

The covenant of Deuteronomy 30 guarantees the return of Israel to the land. The same Israel that would rebel and be cast out of the land and suffer great indignation (De. 28:63-67; 29:22-28) is the Israel that will return (De. 30:1-9).

This covenant was made with the 12 tribes of Israel at the end of the 40 years of wilderness wandering just before they entered the Promised Land. It was made in the land of Moab (De. 29:1), which bordered the land of Canaan on the east.

The covenant is unconditional and sure--"thou SHALT return and shalt obey his voice" (De. 30:2-2); "the Lord thy God WILL bring thee into the land" (De. 30:5); "God WILL circumcise thine heart" (De. 30:6); "God WILL put all these curses upon thine enemies" (De. 30:7); "thou SHALT return and obey the voice of the Lord" (De. 30:8); "God WILL make thee plenteous in every work of thine hand" (De. 30:9).

The covenant will be fulfilled when Israel, scattered among the nations repents (De. 30:1-2). This proves that apostate Israel of the diaspora is the Israel that will fulfill this covenant.

Israel will be gathered from among the nations and brought to "the land which thy fathers possessed" (De. 30:3-5). That land was given to Abraham, Isaac, and Jacob by an eternal covenant.

Israel will be restored to the place of God's blessing. "And the LORD thy God will make thee plenteous in every work of thine hand, in the fruit of thy body, and in the fruit of thy cattle, and in the fruit of thy land, for good: for the LORD will again rejoice over thee for good, as he rejoiced over thy fathers" (De. 30:9).

This covenant is not fulfilled in Israel today, but it will be fulfilled when Israel is converted during the time of Jacob's Trouble (Jeremiah 30:7).

The covenant cannot be applied to "the church" without doing violence to the language. It pertains to people who were scattered among the nations and then brought back to the very land possessed by their fathers. The *same people* who are scattered will be restored.

The Davidic Covenant

The Davidic covenant says God is not finished with Israel (2 Samuel 7:4-17).

The Davidic covenant is an extension of the covenant God made with Abraham. In the Davidic covenant, God gives more details about the national kingdom aspect of the Abrahamic Covenant.

Israel's future existence, restoration to the place of God's favor, and the re-establishment of her kingdom is based on God's unconditional promise to David.

The Davidic Covenant promises the following: First, the house and throne of David will be established forever (2 Sa. 7:13, 16). Second, David's children will be chastised for sin, but the covenant can never be annulled (2 Sa. 7:14-15). Third, the Davidic covenant will be fulfilled through Jesus Christ, David's Son, who inherits David's throne (Mt. 1:1) and who will establish the Davidic kingdom (Isa. 9:6-7).

The Psalmists mention the Davidic covenant and interpret it literally (Ps. 18:50; 89:3-4, 20-37; 132:11-18). The Psalmists teach us that the Davidic Covenant is the means whereby God will establish His kingdom on earth (Ps. 89:20-29). Psalm 72 describes in much detail the physical, earthly kingdom of David's Son Jesus the Messiah.

The prophets often mention the Davidic covenant and interpret it literally (Isa. 9:6-7; 16:5; 22:22-24; 55:3-5; Jer. 23:5-6; 30:9; 33:15-26; Eze. 34:23-24; 37:24-25; Hos. 3:4-5; Amo. 9:11-15; Zec. 12:7 - 13:1).

We look at Amos 9:11-15 and Hosea 3:4-5 later in these studies.

According to Replacement Theology, Jesus is currently sitting on David's throne in heaven and this is the fulfillment of the Davidic covenant, but this requires allegorical gymnastics that I, for one, refuse to engage in. It requires "spiritualizing" the plain words of the Davidic covenant and the New Covenant.

Progressive Dispensationalism also says that Christ is already sitting on David's throne, but it further teaches that Christ will establish a literal 1,000 year kingdom in fulfillment of Old Testament prophecy at His return. This is called "already but not yet," meaning that "Jesus is already on David's throne but has not yet completely fulfilled the promise of God to David for a descendant to sit on his throne" ("What Is Progressive Dispensationalism?" gotquestions.org).

But no verse or passage in the New Testament says that Christ is currently sitting on David's throne. Psalm 110:1-4 doesn't say that; one must read this *into* the passage. David wrote Psalm 110, but he does not say here that the Messiah will sit on his (David's) throne while He awaits victory over His enemies. In fact, the Bible tells us that the throne upon which the Messiah currently sits is the Father's throne.

The New Covenant

The New Covenant says God is not finished with Israel (Jeremiah 31-33).

The New Covenant is God's promise to convert rebellious Israel, restore her to her own land, and bless her.

Consider some facts about the New Covenant:
1. It was made with the nation Israel (Jer. 31:31).
2. It promises the following things:
   a. The New Covenant promises the regathering of Israel (Jer. 31:6-11). Observe that it is the same Israel that was scattered by God among the nations that will be regathered.
   b. The New Covenant promises God's blessing upon Israel's land (Jer. 31:4-5, 12-14, 24-25). Ezekiel often refers to the land as "the land of Israel" when he prophesies of Israel's restoration (Eze. 11:17; 20:38, 42; 37:12; 38:18-19; 40:2; 47:18).
   c. The New Covenant promises the spiritual conversion of the people and cleansing from sin (Jer. 31:33-34).
   d. The New Covenant promises the reestablishment of Israel's kingdom and the possession of the land (Jer. 31:35-37).

e. The New Covenant promises blessing upon Jerusalem as the capital of the kingdom (Jer. 31:38-40).

There is no way to make this fit the church without doing violence to plain Bible language and to clear promises of God.

3. The New Covenant is unconditional and sure (Jer. 33:19-26). God goes out of His way to make this absolutely clear.

> "In those days shall Judah be saved, and Jerusalem shall dwell safely: and this *is the name* wherewith she shall be called, The LORD our righteousness. For thus saith the LORD; David shall never want a man to sit upon the throne of the house of Israel; Neither shall the priests the Levites want a man before me to offer burnt offerings, and to kindle meat offerings, and to do sacrifice continually. And the word of the LORD came unto Jeremiah, saying, Thus saith the LORD; If ye can break my covenant of the day, and my covenant of the night, and that there should not be day and night in their season; *Then* may also my covenant be broken with David my servant, that he should not have a son to reign upon his throne; and with the Levites the priests, my ministers. As the host of heaven cannot be numbered, neither the sand of the sea measured: so will I multiply the seed of David my servant, and the Levites that minister unto me. Moreover the word of the LORD came to Jeremiah, saying, Considerest thou not what this people have spoken, saying, The two families which the LORD hath chosen, he hath even cast them off? thus they have despised my people, that they should be no more a nation before them. Thus saith the LORD; If my covenant *be* not with day and night, *and if* I have not appointed the ordinances of heaven and earth; Then will I cast away the seed of Jacob, and David my servant, *so* that I will not take *any* of his seed *to be* rulers over the seed of Abraham, Isaac, and Jacob: for I will cause their captivity to return, and have mercy on them."

Note that God specifically corrects those who say that He has cast off the families of Israel that they should be no more a nation. This is exactly what Replacement Theology says.

Consider two other major prophecies of the New Covenant in the Old Testament, among many that could be considered:

Isaiah 61:1-12

Isaiah 61:1-2 is the passage that Jesus read in the synagogue at Nazareth at the beginning of His ministry (Lu 4:18-21). He stopped mid-way through verse 2 and said, "This day is this scripture fulfilled in your ears." He didn't read the rest of the prophecy which deals with God's judgment on and the restoration of Israel.

Observe some lessons from the prophecy of Isaiah 61:1-12:

The old wastes will be rebuilt (Isa. 61:4).

Strangers will serve Israel as shepherds, farmers and vinedressers (Isa. 61:5).

Israel will be converted and be the priests and ministers of God (Isa. 61:6). Israel will finally be what God intended that she be, which is a light to the nations.

Israel will be physically blessed and enriched (Isa. 61:6).

The nations will recognize Israel's conversion and know that God has blessed her (Isa. 61:9). This, too, tells us that these are real, earthly events.

Ezekiel 36:22-38

Observe some of the lessons from this major prophecy pertaining to the New Covenant:

God will restore Israel for His name's sake (Eze. 36:22-23). As God's name has been profaned among the nations because of Israel's apostasy, so His name will be glorified in her repentance and restoration. He will be glorified because of the display of His power and He will be glorified because Israel will exhibit His character of holiness and righteousness and truth and compassion before the nations.

72

God will regather Israel from among the nations and bring Israel to her "own land" (Eze. 36:24). This is proof that the land of Israel belongs to ancient Israel and that currently apostate Israel will be restored to it. This is also proof that the same Israel that rejected God and was scattered among the nations is the Israel that will return.

Israel will be converted and cleansed and given a spiritual heart to love and obey God (Eze. 36:25-27).

Israel will then dwell in the land that God gave to their fathers (Eze. 36:28). Again, we see that the land is Israel's for a permanent possession.

Israel will be physically blessed in the land (Eze. 36:29-30, 33-34, 38).

The nations will know that the Lord has done this (Eze. 36:36). The restoration and blessing will be visible, dramatic events, and there will be no question by the onlookers that prophecy will have been fulfilled.

The New Covenant and Church-age Believers

Question: If the New Covenant is not fulfilled in the church, why does the writer of Hebrews quote it (Hebrews 8:6-13; 10:15-19)?

Answer:

1. Hebrews does not say the New Covenant is fulfilled in the church. It twice states, rather, that the New Covenant belongs to "the house of Israel" (Heb. 8:8, 10).

2. Hebrews refers to the New Covenant to show that the Mosaic law was only temporary and that even the Old Testament promised that it would be abolished and replaced by another covenant. Hebrews was written to Jews who professed Christ, some of whom were being tempted to return to the Jewish religion because of persecution. It was written to encourage them that Christ is superior in every way. The writer of Hebrews mentions the New Covenant to show that God had all along planned to replace the Mosaic Covenant with a better one.

3. The writer of Hebrews indicates that the New Testament believer partakes of the *spiritual blessings* of the New Covenant through Christ (Heb. 10:15-18), but nowhere does he say that this covenant has been transferred from national Israel to the church or that the physical aspects of the covenant should be spiritualized. Since the spiritual aspects of the New Covenant (and the spiritual aspects only) are cited in Hebrews 8:8-11 (from Jeremiah 31:31-34), it appears that New Testament believers participate only in the spiritual blessings of the New Covenant through Christ's atonement.

4. The apostle Paul plainly taught that the New Covenant will be fulfilled literally in Israel following the church age (Ro. 11:25-27). In verse 27 Paul refers to the covenant of Jeremiah 31:31-34.

Isaiah 10:20-22

This is one of the many brief passages in the Old Testament prophets that summarize God's dealings with Israel.

The prophecy deals with the remnant of the house of Jacob that will return and be blessed after the judgment. It is a remnant that will be saved, not every Jew or everyone who is the seed of Jacob.

The seed of Jacob will be judged and scattered among the nations, but a remnant of that seed will return and trust Jehovah God "in truth," and the conversion with "overflow with righteousness." This has not yet happened, but it will happen during the time of Jacob's trouble when Israel will be converted in preparation for and in conjunction with the return of Christ and the establishment of His kingdom.

Ezekiel 34:11-31

This beautiful prophecy of the Shepherd leaves no doubt that God is not finished with national Israel.

The Shepherd, of course, is Jehovah God, and we know from the New Testament that this is Christ, the Son of God who identified Himself as the Good Shepherd (Joh. 10:11, 14).

He will regather the sheep from the countries where they have been scattered and bring them to "their own land, and feed them upon the mountains of Israel" (Eze. 34:12-13). This obviously is not what God is doing today in the church age. This is national Israel being brought back from her Diaspora to her own land.

God will distinguish between "cattle and cattle" (Eze. 34:17-22). Not every Jew will be saved. Zechariah explains that one-third of the Jews living at that time will be saved (Zec. 13:8-9).

The Lord will be their God, and David will be a prince among them (Eze. 34:24). David's Son, Immanuel or Jehovah God in the flesh, will sit on the throne of Israel.

God will make a new covenant with Israel, and she will experience peace and blessing and prosperity (Eze. 34:25-29).

Note that the God plainly says that "the house of Israel are my people" (Eze. 34:30). This refers to restored Israel in the future.

Ezekiel 37:1-14

The prophecy of the Valley of Dry Bones says God is not finished with Israel (Ezekiel 37).

This great prophecy is the only one that explains that Israel will return from her wanderings among the nations in two stages, and in the first stage she will return in a spiritually dead condition.

The interpretation of the valley of dry bones is plainly given in the prophecy itself. It signifies Israel in her dispersion among the nations.

"Then he said unto me, Son of man, these bones are the whole house of Israel: behold, they say, Our bones are dried,

75

and our hope is lost: we are cut off for our parts" (Eze. 37:11).

The resurrection of the dry bones represents Israel's return to the land and restoration as a nation.

> "Therefore prophesy and say unto them, Thus saith the Lord GOD; Behold, O my people, I will open your graves, and cause you to come up out of your graves, and bring you into the land of Israel" (Eze. 37:12).

This is as great a miracle as the resurrection from the dead. Never in human history has a nation been evicted from its land and scattered throughout the world for 2,000 years to survive as a nation and be restored to its original land with its original language and religion.

The first stage of the restoration of Israel is in an unconverted state.

> "So I prophesied as I was commanded: and as I prophesied, there was a noise, and behold a shaking, and the bones came together, bone to his bone. And when I beheld, lo, the sinews and the flesh came up upon them, and the skin covered them above: BUT THERE WAS NO BREATH IN THEM" (Eze. 37:7-8).

This is exactly *what* Israel is today and *where* Israel is today prophetically. Modern Israel is not righteous and is not a fulfillment of the regathering described in connection with the prophecies we have previously considered that describe the New Covenant. Since the 20th century, the land of Israel has been developed in an amazing way, but it is not a fulfillment of prophecies about the desert blossoming as the rose (Isaiah 35:1). Modern Israel is, by her own profession, a secular state and most Jews are secular Jews who aren't religious and don't believe in the God of the Bible. A large percentage of them are atheists or agnostics. A minority hold to various branches of "orthodox Judaism," which is a religion that does not follow the Old Testament but rather follows the Talmud. "Rabbinic Judaism" is ancient Phariseeism.

Israel is back in the land in an apostate condition to set the stage for the fulfillment of the last week of Daniel's 70 Week prophecy (Da. 9:27). Israel must return in a spiritually dead condition in order to sign a covenant with the Antichrist. A living, redeemed Israel would not do that.

But Ezekiel's prophecy explains that God is going to touch Israel *again* and convert her spiritually.

> "Then said he unto me, Prophesy unto the wind, prophesy, son of man, and say to the wind, Thus saith the Lord GOD; Come from the four winds, O breath, and breathe upon these slain, that they may live. So I prophesied as he commanded me, and the breath came into them, and they lived, and stood up upon their feet, an exceeding great army. ... And shall put my spirit in you, and ye shall live, and I shall place you in your own land: then shall ye know that I the LORD have spoken it, and performed it, saith the LORD" (Eze. 37:9-10, 14).

This is in the future, and it is described in many prophecies, as we have seen, such as Zechariah 12-14.

It is clear from Ezekiel's prophecy that God is not finished with Israel. The same apostate Israel that was evicted from the land and scattered among her nations for her sin will be restored to the land. This has nothing to do with church age saints.

Ezekiel 37:15-28

This prophecy emphasizes that Israel and Judah will be reunited (Eze. 37:15-20). Though most Jews today do not know their tribe for certain, God knows, and He doesn't need a DNA test. The 12 tribes are not lost and will be restored by God.

Israel will be regathered from the nations and brought into "their own land" (Eze. 37:21). They "will dwell in the land that I have given unto Jacob my servant, wherein your fathers have dwelt" (Eze. 37:25). There can be no question that the prophecy predicts the restoration of Israel to her own land and that it is presented as a literal, physical event.

Israel will be one nation and have one king and prince (Eze. 37:22, 24, 25). David himself will be there in a leadership position, but other Scriptures explain that it is David's Son who will be the King of kings.

Israel will be cleansed of her sin and will obey God (Eze. 37:23, 24).

God will make an everlasting covenant with Israel (Eze. 37:26).

God will place His temple in their midst (Eze. 37:26-27). This is the temple described in great detail in Ezekiel 40-48.

These things will be seen by the nations and God will be glorified by them (Eze. 37:28). The prophet is describing real physical, earthly events.

Ezekiel 38-39

The prophecy of Gog and Magog says that God is not finished with Israel (Ezekiel 38-39).

This prophecy describes an attack upon Israel by a great military alliance from the north.

Our purpose here is not to look at the prophecy in detail but to see that it proves that God is not finished with Israel.

The prophecy occurs when Israel has been "brought back from the sword" and "is brought forth out of the nations" (Eze. 38:8). It occurs after a regathering that follows the land of Israel becoming waste. Obviously it refers to the restoration of the same Israel that was scattered among the nations.

The attack of Gog and Magog will occur in the latter days (Eze. 38:16). We see that Israel still exists in the end times.

The attack will occur at a time when the "people of Israel dwelleth safely" (Eze. 38:14). This isn't today. It could be during the first 3.5 years of her covenant with the Antichrist. It could refer to after Armageddon. It's difficult to place the time exactly, but it is certainly referring to a literal Israel in a literal land.

The armies of Gog and Magog will be supernaturally destroyed by God (Eze. 38:21-22).

Israel will be brought back from the nations and will know the Lord. God's Spirit will be poured upon "the house of Israel" (Eze. 39:25-29).

The nations will then understand God's dealings with Israel (Eze. 39:23).

In this prophecy, God calls Israel "my people" (Eze. 38:14, 16). The land is called "my land" (Eze. 38:16), referring to Jehovah God, and "the land of Israel" (Eze. 38:18, 19) and "their own land" (Eze. 39:28).

It is perfectly obvious that God is not finished with Israel, though she is presently apostate, that she will return to the land, be restored to God and to the place of His blessing, and her enemies will be punished.

It is impossible to apply this prophecy to the church without doing grave injustice to the principle of the literal interpretation of Scripture.

Ezekiel 40-48

The prophecy of the Millennial Temple says God is not finished with Israel (Ezekiel 40-48).

This amazing prophecy describes in great detail the temple that will be built during Christ's millennial reign and the allotment of the land to the 12 tribes of Israel. There is nothing here that applies to the church except by indirect application.

The temple will reside at the heart of a holy area about 47 miles square (Eze. 48:20). Within this area will be a portion reserved for the priests and a portion belonging to the Levites

(Eze. 45:3-45; 48:10-13). The rest of the 47 mile square will be for the city and its suburbs (Eze. 48:15). Beyond this 47 mile square is a portion for the prince (Eze. 45:7; 48:21-22).

The topography of the area will be changed dramatically to accommodate these things.

The temple will sit on the top of a high mountain and will thus be the prominent feature of the region (Eze. 40:2; 43:12).

Glorious in composition, it will be filled with Christ's glorious light (Eze. 44:4).

Christ will enter the eastern gate of the temple in His splendid glory accompanied by the cherubims (Eze. 43:1-4; 44:4).

Those who interpret Bible prophecy allegorically claim that the temple described by Ezekiel is not a literal future temple. We do not accept this view for the following reasons:

1. The temple is described in a very literal sense. There is nothing in the prophecy to indicate that it is symbolic. The temple is described in great detail in the same sense that God described the tabernacle. There are 318 precise measurements and the use of 37 unique architectural terms (e.g., doorposts, windows, arches, stairs, pillars, settles).

2. God specifically gave this prophecy as a witness to the nation Israel in her unbelief (Eze. 43:10-11). If the prophecy somehow symbolically described "the church" instead of Israel, God's statement through Ezekiel would make no sense.

3. Other prophets describe this same temple. In fact, the Millennial Temple is a major theme of Bible prophecy. See Isaiah 2:2-3; 56:6-7; 60:7, 13; Jeremiah 33:17-18; Ezekiel 37:26-28; 40-48; Joel 3:18; Haggai 2:7-9; Zechariah 1:16; 6:12-15; 14:20; Malachi 3:1-5.

4. The prophecy even names the priests who will be in charge (Eze. 44:15; 48:11) and describes their work in detail (44:17-26). Allegories and parables do not use the names of real people.

Consider some difficulties pertaining to the Millennial Temple examined:

1. Those who hold to replacement theology object to the reinstitution of the animal sacrifices, claiming that these have been done away in Christ (Hebrews 10:8-10).

Answer: The sacrifices are emphasized in Ezekiel 40-48 by great repetition. "Offering" is mentioned 61 times and "blood" is mentioned five times. Other prophets describe the reinstitution of the sacrifices (Ps. 51:18-19; 60:7; Isa. 66:21; Jer. 33:17-18; Zec. 14:21; Hag. 2:9; Mal. 3:3-4). The sacrifices will be powerful visual reminders of Christ's sacrifice.

> "Christians have the Lord's Supper, and in it they show the Lord's death with perfect acceptance. But we do not permit any sacrificial efficacy to be attached to that memorial ... Nor will the enlightened Israelite (and they will all be thus enlightened) in the future permit any atoning efficacy to be attached to those sacrifices; they will also be memorials, and only memorials, of that same all-sufficient offering of Christ crucified. ... The entire absence of the veil in that future Temple will be evidence enough of the sacrifices being memorials and not propitiations" (F.C. Jennings, *Studies in Isaiah*).

We see here that Israel is not the Church. While the church has no such sacrifices, having the ordinances of the Lord's Supper and baptism to remind us of Christ's sacrifice, Israel has a different program. Her sacrifices will be reinstated, but the people will understand their true meaning. The sacrifices will be a powerful symbolic witness of the gospel to the nations during the Millennium. The Gentiles who will come to Jerusalem from throughout the earth (Isa. 2:2-3) will be instructed by the sacrifices accompanied by the teaching of the priests.

2. The temple and environs cannot fit into present-day Israel. The temple area itself will be about a mile square (500 reeds plus 50 cubits, Eze. 45:2), which is larger than Jerusalem today. The area that will contain the temple, the

land reserved for the prince and the priests, the city of Jerusalem and its suburbs, will be about 49 miles square (25,000 x 25,000 reeds, Eze. 48:8 20). (The reed is six large cubits long, each cubit being 21 inches, which equals 126 inches or 10.5 feet, Eze. 40:5.) This is an area greater than the area between the Mediterranean Sea and the Jordan River today.

Answer: Many commentators measure the holy area by cubits rather than reeds, since the word "reeds" in Ezekiel 45:1 and 48:8 is supplied by the translators. 25,000 cubits would be about 8.3 miles.

Either way, God will make it work. The Bible says that the topography of Jerusalem and Israel will be dramatically changed at the coming of Christ. See Ezekiel 38:22; Zechariah 14:4, 10; Revelation 16:18-19. It also says that Israel will be enlarged (Isa. 49:18-21).

3. Who is the prince who will have children (Eze. 46:18) and offer sacrifices (Eze. 46:12)?

Answer: It could refer to David (Eze. 34:23-24; 37:24-25; Jer. 33:25-26). When it speaks of "his sons" in Ezekiel 46:18, it does not necessarily mean the prince will conceive children. It could be referring, instead, to the Israelites as his sons. Thus, this could be, and probably is, the resurrected David himself.

4. The prophecy refers to the keeping of the sabbath, but that has been done away in Christ (Eze. 46:1; Col. 2:16-17).

Answer: The sabbath was given to the nation Israel as an everlasting sign (Ex. 31:13; Eze. 20:12). Again, it is necessary to understand that Israel and the church have different programs.

Daniel's 70 Week Prophecy

Daniel's 70 Week prophecy says that God is not finished with Israel (Daniel 9:24-28).

This great prophecy gives a complete summary of God's program for Israel from the Babylonian Captivity until the return of Christ. The 70 weeks are weeks of years, or 490 years, as it is clear from the fulfillment so far.

During the 70 weeks, God's judgments upon Israel will be completed and Christ will return to bring in the kingdom. The angel tells Daniel that the prophecy pertains to his own people, the Jews, and to the holy city, Jerusalem (Da. 9:24).

The first 69 weeks (483 years) extended from the time that the commandment was given to rebuild Jerusalem after the Babylonian captivity to the time of Christ's first coming. The commandment to rebuild the walls of Jerusalem was given by Artaxerxes the king of Persia, and is described in Nehemiah 1:1-8. (The same king gave the commandment to rebuild the temple 13 years earlier as described in the book of Ezra, but Daniel 9:25 speaks particularly of the rebuilding of the city wall.) Daniel's prophecy describes three great events that occurred in this time. First, Jerusalem was rebuilt (Da. 9:25). The rebuilding of the city streets and walls in troublous times is described in the book of Nehemiah. Second, Messiah was "cut off, but not for himself," meaning that He died on the cross for man's sins (Da. 9:26). His death was substitutionary. Third, the city and temple were destroyed (Da. 9:26). This occurred in AD 70 when the armies of Rome destroyed Jerusalem.

After that there will continue to be wars until the time of the end (Da. 9:26). This describes the Roman Jewish wars, but it also describes the last 2,000 years of Israel's history. Even today, though Israel is back in the land, she has had no peace, and she will have no peace until she repents and receives her Messiah, Jesus.

The last week, or seven years, of Daniel's prophecy remains to be fulfilled (Da. 9:27). Between the 69th and 70th weeks is the church age, which is called a "mystery" because it was not revealed to the Old Testament prophets (Eph. 3:3-6). The church age is like a valley that the Old Testament prophets did not see lying between the peaks of the first and second coming of Christ. Paul describes the church age as the time of Israel's blindness in Romans 11:25-27.

The last week (seven years) of Daniel's prophecy is divided into two parts (Da. 9:27). At the beginning of the seven years, the Antichrist will make a false peace covenant with Israel. It is at this time that the Jewish temple will be rebuilt in Jerusalem. Revelation 11 describes it being measured (Re. 11:1-2) at the very time when the Two Witnesses will prophesy in Jerusalem. Mid-way through the seven years the Antichrist will break this covenant and desecrate the temple by exalting himself as God. Compare 2 Thessalonians 2:3-4. This event marks the beginning of the 3.5 years of Great Tribulation. Jesus calls this event "the abomination of desolation" (Mt. 24:15).

This prophecy sees Israel, Daniel's people, continuing to the time of the Antichrist. It teaches us that the Antichrist and his program does not pertain to the church; it pertains to Israel and to her land and temple.

Hosea

Hosea 3:4-5 says that God is not finished with Israel. This passage plainly describes the fall of Israel *followed by her return* and the re-establishment of the Davidic kingdom.

> "For the children of Israel shall abide many days without a king, and without a prince, and without a sacrifice, and without an image, and without an ephod, and *without* teraphim: **AFTERWARD** shall the children of Israel return, and seek the LORD their God, and David their king; and shall fear the LORD and his goodness in the latter days" (Ho. 3:4-5).

This is the Bible's teaching about Israel and her future in a nutshell. Israel would rebel against God's Word, be judged, abide many days without a king or a sacrifice or a priesthood (e.g., no kingdom and no temple), then the same Israel will return, repent, and be restored and blessed. The restoration will occur "in the latter days."

Amos

Amos says that God is not finished with Israel.

> "Behold, the eyes of the Lord GOD *are* upon the sinful kingdom, and I will destroy it from off the face of the earth; saving that I will not utterly destroy the house of Jacob, saith the LORD. For, lo, I will command, and I will sift the house of Israel among all nations, like as *corn* is sifted in a sieve, yet shall not the least grain fall upon the earth. All the sinners of my people shall die by the sword, which say, The evil shall not overtake nor prevent us. In that day will I raise up the tabernacle of David that is fallen, and close up the breaches thereof; and I will raise up his ruins, and I will build it as in the days of old: That they may possess the remnant of Edom, and of all the heathen, which are called by my name, saith the LORD that doeth this. Behold, the days come, saith the LORD, that the plowman shall overtake the reaper, and the treader of grapes him that soweth seed; and the mountains shall drop sweet wine, and all the hills shall melt. And I will bring again the captivity of my people of Israel, and they shall build the waste cities, and inhabit *them*; and they shall plant vineyards, and drink the wine thereof; they shall also make gardens, and eat the fruit of them. And I will plant them upon their land, and they shall no more be pulled up out of their land which I have given them, saith the LORD thy God" (Am. 9:8-15).

This is another of the many Old Testament prophecies of the restoration of Israel after her worldwide dispersion. It is clear and precise, and only by doing violence to the language can it be made to describe anything other than a restoration of the nation Israel.

Consider some of the lessons from a literal interpretation of this prophecy:

God will judge Israel severely for her sin, but He will not utterly destroy her (Am. 9:8).

Israel will be sifted among the nations, but not the least grain will fall to the earth (Am. 9:9). God has had His eye upon Israel and has been in control of her wanderings, though she is in a condition of disobedience and spiritual blindness.

The sinners of Israel who do not believe God's Word will perish (Am. 9:10). They are the national seed of Abraham, but that does not mean they are saved or will be saved. Those who do not repent will not be saved.

But Israel itself will be restored. The tabernacle of David will be raised up and built as in the old days (Am. 9:11). This will occur when Christ returns and sits on the throne of David, ruling Israel and the whole world.

The restoration of the house of David will be accompanied by blessings on the land (Am. 9:13-15). The prophecy pertains to *a land*. And note that God twice says it is "THEIR LAND." As we have seen, God gave it to Abraham, Isaac, and Jacob. God said to Jacob, "And the land which I gave Abraham and Isaac, to thee I will give it, and to thy seed after thee will I give the land" (Ge. 35:9-12). To national Israel belongs the land that was promised to Abraham. Compare Genesis 12:7; 13:14-17; 15:7. In 1 Chronicles 16:13-16, David affirmed that Abraham's covenant passed through Isaac and Jacob to Jacob's children, national Israel, and that the promise includes the inheritance of the land.

Words could not be more clear and simple to understand, and this is the consistent testimony of the entire Bible. The *same Israel* that turned from God and was judged and scattered among the nations will be restored to her own land, the very land upon which she lived in ancient times, and she will live in that land and be blessed in that land, and the Son of David will restore the Davidic kingdom and rule and reign over it. This is the teaching of the Bible from the Pentateuch to Revelation.

Amos' prophecy is cited by James in Acts 15.

> "And to this agree the words of the prophets; as it is written, After this I will return, and will build again the tabernacle of David, which is fallen down; and I will build again the ruins thereof, and I will set it up: That the residue of men might seek after the Lord, and all the Gentiles, upon whom my name is called, saith the Lord, who doeth all these things" (Ac. 15:15-17).

Here James quotes Amos 9:11 and gives a general reference to Amos 9:12 without quoting it exactly. His simple point is that the Old Testament prophets foresaw God's blessing on the Gentiles. This was the subject in question at the Jerusalem conference.

James does not say that Amos 9 is fulfilled in the church or that God is finished with Israel. For that, it would have been necessary that he interpret the kingdom prophecies allegorically or spiritually, but instead he interprets Amos literally. Since he cites the part of the prophecy about the salvation of the Gentiles as literal, there is no reason to believe that he was looking at the restoration of the house of David as anything other than literal.

If the apostles had believed that the church has fulfilled such prophecies, this would have been the ideal place to have made that perfectly clear, but they did just the opposite.

Zechariah

Zechariah says God is not finished with Israel.

Consider the great prophecy of Zechariah 12-14.

Jerusalem will be besieged by the "people of the earth" but will be delivered and will conquer all their armies (Zec. 12: 1-9). The nations that come against Jerusalem will be destroyed. This has never happened. God destroyed Sennacherib's army, but that consisted of one Assyrian army, not the nations of the world. The armies of the world have never attacked Israel before. Zechariah's prophecy will be fulfilled when the nations attack Israel during the time of the Antichrist. It is part of the Battle of Armageddon.

At that time, Israel will repent and will acknowledge the crucified Jesus as Christ (Zec. 12:10-14). They will look upon him "whom they have pierced, and they shall mourn for him, as one mourneth for his only son." The mourning will be in Jerusalem and all over Israel. The mourning will involve the house of David and the house of Levi and the other families. This is obviously talking about national Israel and not the church in any sense. Israelites today might not know their tribal genealogies, but God knows.

Israel will be cleansed by the blood of Christ (Zec. 13:1). Those who are cleansed are described as "the house of David," which is certainly not the church.

Israel will be cleansed of idolatry and false teaching (Zec. 13:2-6).

One-third of Israel will be converted, and two-thirds will be judged (Zec. 13:7-9). The third part will be brought through the Great Tribulation for purifying (Zec. 13:9). This is why the tribulation is also called the time of Jacob's trouble (Jer. 30:7).

At that time God will say, "It is my people" (Zec. 13:9). This does not refer to church-age believers. It refers to Israel, the very Israel that goes through the fire of tribulation.

The Lord will return to the Mount of Olives and it will be divided (Zec. 14:1-7). A great valley will be formed, and the remnant of Jews will flee from Jerusalem.

A river of living waters will flow from Jerusalem (Zec. 14:8). Ezekiel also describes this, and it will heal the Dead Sea and the desert area in the Judean wilderness to the east of Jerusalem (Eze. 47:8-12).

Israel's topography will be changed (Zec. 14:10).

The LORD will be king over all the earth (Zec. 14:9). His kingship of the earth is spoken of in the context of His return to the Mount of Olives and blessings on the land of Israel.

Israel will be blessed and enriched (Zec. 14:14).

The surviving nations will come to Jerusalem to worship the King, the LORD of hosts (Zec. 14:16).

The nations that refuse to submit will be punished (Zec. 14:17-19).

Israel will be perfectly holy (Zec. 14:20-21).

This prophecy cannot be spiritualized to refer to the church without doing it such damage that it is rendered meaningless.

Christ's Teaching

The Lord Jesus taught that God is not finished with Israel. Consider four examples:

In **Matthew 23**, after Christ condemned the Pharisees and their false traditions and false works religion, He said to the Jews of that day and to Jerusalem, "Behold, your house is left unto you desolate. For I say unto you, Ye shall not see me henceforth, **TILL** ye shall say, Blessed is he that cometh in the name of the Lord" (Matthew 23:38-39). Note the word "till." Christ promised judgment upon Israel. He prophesied that their temple would be desolate. But the judgment wasn't going to be permanent. It has an end, and it will end when Israel repents. This repentance is described in great detail by the prophet Zechariah (chapter 12).

In **Matthew 24**, Christ continued this same teaching. The temple of His day would be destroyed so that there would not remain "one stone upon another, that shall not be thrown down" (verse 2). The visitor to Jerusalem can still see the "Titus stones" that were thrown from the temple mount in AD 70 and crashed to the street below at the south end of the western wall. And Jesus prophesied of the rise of the Antichrist spoken of by Daniel, who will stand in a rebuilt Jewish temple (Mt. 24:15). And then those who are in Judea will flee (Mt. 24:16). Jesus is prophesying of the Israel that exists today, the Israel that occupies the hills of Judea and is preparing to build the third temple. Christ is prophesying of modern Israel. He says she will still be under God's judgment in the end times and will endure great tribulation (Mt. 24:41). He prophesies of false Jewish christs that will rise, and we know that many of them have already risen (Mt. 24:24-26).

In Matthew 24, Christ is teaching the same literal truths about Israel that all of the prophets describe. He doesn't describe Israel's conversion in Matthew 24, but that is described in many other prophecies. All of the prophecies give the same literal plan for Israel: rejection of Jesus as Christ, dispersion, judgment, conversion, restoration.

What about Matthew 21:43?

> "Therefore say I unto you, The kingdom of God shall be taken from you, and given to a nation bringing forth the fruits thereof."

If this verse were isolated, it could teach that God was finished with Israel and that the church has replaced Israel, but it cannot possibly teach that since Christ Himself said that He is not finished with Israel. He said they would not see Him TILL they repent (Mt. 23:39).

Christ always described a literal physical kingdom on earth. He said "They shall come from the east, and from the west, and from the north, and from the south, and shall sit down in the kingdom of God (Lu. 13:29).

Christ gave the parable in **Luke 19:11-27** specifically to teach that the kingdom of God would not come at that time but would come after the king would go into a far country and then return (Lu. 19:12). After he returns he will reward his servants and judge his enemies. This describes the church age followed by the establishment of an earthly kingdom, exactly as we see throughout Scripture.

Acts 1 also tells us that Christ taught that the kingdom of Israel will be restored.

After His resurrection, He spoke to the disciples "of the things pertaining to the kingdom of God" (Ac. 1:3).

It is obvious that the kingdom Christ taught them about was the kingdom promised in Old Testament prophecy and that He had not taught them that the church has replaced Israel, because just before He ascended, the disciples asked, "Lord, wilt thou at this time restore again the kingdom to Israel?" (Ac. 1:6).

They believed that Israel's kingdom would be restored, they just didn't know *when*.

Christ's reply makes it doubly clear that they were all on the same page about the future of Israel's kingdom. He said,

> "It is not for you to know the times or the seasons, which the Father hath put in his own power. But ye shall receive power, after that the Holy Ghost is come upon you: and ye shall be witnesses unto me both in Jerusalem, and in all Judaea, and in Samaria, and unto the uttermost part of the earth" (Ac. 1:7-8).

If the disciples had still misunderstood Christ's teaching about Israel's kingdom, this would have been the perfect time to have corrected their thinking. But Christ didn't say, "You are confused; there is no restoration of Israel's kingdom." Instead, He told them that the timing of the re-establishment of the kingdom is God's business, and they need to focus on their own business in this present time, which is preaching the gospel to the ends of the earth.

Acts 15

The apostolic conference in Acts 15 says that God is not finished with Israel.

The conference was for the purpose of deciding the issue of whether Gentile believers must follow the law of Moses (Acts 15:1).

The determination by the apostles and prophets was that they are not so obligated, because the law of Moses was a heavy yoke, whereas salvation is by God grace (Acts 15:10-11).

They understood that the purpose of the present time or age or dispensation is for God to take out of the Gentiles a people for His name (Acts 15:14). That is a description of the church age in a nutshell. Elsewhere Paul speaks of the fulness of the Gentiles coming in (Ro. 11:25). This tells us that there is an end to the church as far as who will belong to it. There is no end to the church (Eph. 3:21), but there is an end to the *church age* during which the church is being gathered together. The *church age* has a beginning and an end.

In his summary, James shows that this is conformable to the teaching of the Old Testament prophets. He quotes from Amos to show that the prophets taught that God would restore the house of David after it was fallen down and would rebuild its ruins, *and at that time there would be Gentiles who call on the name of the Lord* (Amos 9:11-12). James is not saying that the house of David is restored in the church. To the contrary, he is saying that it will be restored in the future and that when it is restored there will exist saved Gentiles. That implies the salvation of Gentiles *before* the restoration of Israel's kingdom, which hints at the church age. This does not contradict the teaching that the church is a mystery. It is a mystery and was nowhere revealed in Old Testament prophecy, yet there are hints of the church age in the Old Testament that can now be understood in hindsight.

What is indisputable is that the apostles believed that the kingdom of David would be literally restored, and it will be restored in the future and it is *not* currently restored in the church age.

The apostles interpreted the prophecy of Amos 9:8-15 literally.

Romans 11

Paul says in Romans 11 that God is not finished with Israel.

This passage clearly teaches that God is not finished with Israel and that the church has not replaced Israel.

As there is a casting away of Israel, so there will be a receiving of Israel which will be associated with the resurrection of the dead (Ro. 11:15). Daniel also associates the restoration of Israel with the resurrection (Da. 12:1-2).

The church, though different from Israel, is closely associated with spiritual Israel (Ro. 11:16-24).

- The root is not Israel herself. The root is Abraham's covenant and Abraham's Seed Jesus Christ. Both the church and Israel are connected with this root. There is one tree and multiple branches. An Old Testament saint like Samuel and a New Testament saint like Apollos are both children of Abraham. Some of the natural branches growing from the root were broken off because of unbelief, and when they repent they will be grafted back in. The natural branches refer to Israel by nature; the Jews are by nature the children of Abraham, but the natural cannot inherit the spiritual kingdom of God.

- Professing Christians, too, should fear lest they be found to be in unbelief (Ro. 11:20-21). This is the same type of warning as in Hebrews 3:12 - 4:3. It is a warning about professing Christ without possessing Christ through saving faith.

Blindness in part is happened to Israel until the fulness of the Gentiles be come in (Ro. 11:25-27). This is the New Testament teaching about the church and the church age and Israel in a nutshell. Israel is in spiritual blindness today, and that is what we see in modern Israel, but God isn't finished with blind Israel. She will be saved and converted, and God's covenants with her will be fulfilled. Words could not be plainer.

When Paul says that "all Israel shall be saved," he is referring to Israel as Israel and not to every Israelite. This is clear in comparing Scripture with Scripture. All Israel will be saved in the sense of the 12 tribes. Ezekiel tells us that God will restore Judah and Israel and they will be one (Eze. 37:15-20). But Zechariah tells us that only one-third of individual Israelites living in that day will be converted (Zec. 13:8-9). Elsewhere, Paul stated that a remnant of Israel will be saved (Ro. 9:27).

The Book of Revelation

Finally, the book of Revelation says that God is not finished with Israel.

In fact, the book of Revelation can be outlined according to a distinction between the church and Israel. In chapters 1-3, the churches are addressed, but in Revelation 4:1, John is caught up to heaven and after that we don't see the churches on earth.

In Revelation 7, 12,000 individuals from each of 12 tribes of Israel are sealed (Re. 7:1-8). The names of the tribes are given. Here we see that the 12 tribes of Israel have not ceased to exist before God and that He knows who and where they are and they have a future in His prophetic plan. The witness for God in the earth during the Tribulation is Israel, not the church.

In Revelation 8, the prayers of the saints are prayers for judgment. Only Israel prayed such prayers. Church-age saints are instructed to pray *for* her enemies, not *against* them (Lu. 9:51-56). The imprecatory prayers of Revelation are those of the Psalms and are based on God's promise to Abraham to curse those that cursed him and his seed (Ge. 12:1-3).

In Revelation 9, the scorpion-like creatures are given freedom to hurt all earth-dwellers except those Jews who were sealed by the angel of Revelation 7. If church-age believers were on earth, they would be subject to this horrible judgment of God.

Revelation 10 identifies the events of Revelation 4-18 with those foretold by Old Testament prophets--the days of the

Great Tribulation, the "Day of the Lord." The church age was never in the view of these Old Testament prophecies; it was a mystery not yet revealed. The church has a different purpose and program than national Israel. It is Israel that is in view in Old Testament prophecy and in Revelation 4-18.

The ministry of the two witnesses of Revelation 11 identifies them with national Israel and with Old Testament prophecies of the *"Day of the Lord."* The two witnesses minister from Jerusalem, Israel's capital. The church has no such capital, her hope being heavenly, not earthly (Col. 3:1-4; Php. 3:17-21). The two witnesses are associated with the rebuilt Jewish temple, which is measured at the beginning of the prophecy, telling us that this is when it will be built. The two witnesses are clothed in sackcloth, which speaks of Israel. The sackcloth signifies repentance from sin and sorrow because of some calamity (1 Ki. 21:27; 2 Ki. 19:1; Est. 4:1; Isa. 15:3; Jer. 4:8). Nowhere are the churches seen in sackcloth. The churches are told, rather, to *"rejoice in the Lord alway"* (Php. 4:4). The church-age believer's judgment is forever past, and he is to keep his mind centered in the heavenlies where, positionally, he is already seated with Christ (Eph. 2:5-10). Revelation 11:4 identifies the two witnesses with the Old Testament prophecy of Zechariah 4:3, 11, 14. Further, the two witnesses call down judgment upon their enemies in Revelation 10:5-6. Jesus rebuked his disciples for desiring to do just this and instructed the church-age believer to pray for the well-being of his enemies, not for their destruction (Lu. 9:54-56; Ro. 12:14, 17-21). None of this is church ground. This is Israel ground. This is literal Jerusalem, literal Jewish temple ground.

The devil persecutes Israel, not the church, during the Tribulation (Re. 12). There can be no doubt that the woman in this chapter signifies Israel. Verse 5 shows the woman bringing forth Christ, and it is obvious that Jesus was brought forth by Israel, not by the church (Isa. 9:6-7; Ro. 9:5). Also, the symbols of Revelation 12:1-2 recall familiar Old

Testament typology of Israel. She is referred to as a woman (Isa. 54:5-7). The sun and moon and the 12 stars of verse 2 bring us directly to Joseph's dream regarding Israel (Ge. 37:9). The words of Revelation 12:2 are almost an exact quote from Micah 5:3, speaking of Israel's delivery of the Messiah. These symbols are not used in the New Testament to refer to the churches.

Proof Texts of Replacement Theology

Having seen in the last chapter that the Bible consistently and repeatedly teaches that God is not finished with the nation Israel and that the church has not replaced Israel, let's examine some major proof texts that are used to support Replacement Theology.

Briefly, Replacement Theology takes a few verses out of context and uses them to overthrow the teaching of the entire Bible. This, of course, is the standard operation procedure of false teaching.

Matthew 21:43 - "Therefore say I unto you, The kingdom of God shall be taken from you, and given to a nation bringing forth the fruits thereof."

If this verse were isolated, it could teach that God was finished with Israel and that the church has replaced Israel, but it cannot possibly teach that since Christ Himself said that He is not finished with Israel.

He said Israel would not see Him TILL they repent (Mt. 23:39).

Christ always described a literal physical kingdom on earth. He said "They shall come from the east, and from the west, and from the north, and from the south, and shall sit down in the kingdom of God (Lu. 13:29).

Christ gave the parable in **Luke 19:11-27** specifically to teach that the kingdom of God would not come at that time but would come after the king would go into a far country and then return (Lu. 19:12). After he returns he will reward his servants and judge his enemies. This describes the church age followed by the establishment of an earthly kingdom, exactly as we see throughout Scripture.

Acts 1 also tells us that Christ taught that the kingdom of Israel will be restored.

After His resurrection, He spoke to the disciples "of the things pertaining to the kingdom of God" (Ac. 1:3).

It is obvious that the kingdom Christ taught them about was the kingdom promised in Old Testament prophecy and that He had not taught them that the church has replaced Israel, because just before He ascended, the disciples asked, "Lord, wilt thou at this time restore again the kingdom to Israel?" (Ac. 1:6).

They believed that Israel's kingdom would be restored, they just didn't know *when*.

Christ's reply makes it doubly clear that they were all on the same page about the future of Israel's kingdom. He said,

> "It is not for you to know the times or the seasons, which the Father hath put in his own power. But ye shall receive power, after that the Holy Ghost is come upon you: and ye shall be witnesses unto me both in Jerusalem, and in all Judaea, and in Samaria, and unto the uttermost part of the earth" (Ac. 1:7-8).

If the disciples had still misunderstood Christ's teaching about Israel's kingdom, this would have been the perfect time to have corrected their thinking. But Christ didn't say, "You are confused; there is no restoration of Israel's kingdom." Instead, He told them that the timing of the re-establishment of the kingdom is God's business, and they need to focus on their own business in this present time, which is preaching the gospel to the ends of the earth.

John 8:39-42 - "They answered and said unto him, Abraham is our father. Jesus saith unto them, If ye were Abraham's children, ye would do the works of Abraham. But now ye seek to kill me, a man that hath told you the truth, which I have heard of God: this did not Abraham. Ye do the deeds of your father. Then said they to him, We be not born of fornication; we have one Father, even God. Jesus said unto them, If God were your Father, ye would

love me: for I proceeded forth and came from God; neither came I of myself, but he sent me."

Here Christ shows the Jews that not all of Abraham's children are His true spiritual children. It is obvious that the Jews were Abraham's physical children, but by rejecting Jesus as the Christ they proved that they were not his spiritual children.

Yet this passage says nothing about Christians being the true Israel.

Romans 2:28-29 - "For he is not a Jew, which is one outwardly; neither is that circumcision, which is outward in the flesh: But he is a Jew, which is one inwardly; and circumcision is that of the heart, in the spirit, and not in the letter; whose praise is not of men, but of God."

Here Paul was showing the Jews of his day that their outward conformity to the law was not true righteousness and could not save them. Romans 2:28-29 is a simple statement that the true Jew, meaning the Jew that pleases God, the Jew that God intended when He made the Jews, is not one who merely observes the outward rituals of the Old Testament. Rather, he is one who is circumcised in the heart and loves God and His Word, as Abraham, Samuel, David, Deborah, Jeremiah, and Mary and Joseph.

This is not saying that an unsaved Jew is not a Jew or that unsaved Israel is not Israel. It is certainly not saying that a Christian is the true Jew and that the church is Israel. All such things have to be read into the passage.

Romans 9:6 - "Not as though the word of God hath taken none effect. For they are not all Israel, which are of Israel."

The context of this statement is found in verses 1-8. Paul is expressing his love for Israel even in her unbelieving condition. He recounts her great benefits in having the covenants and the law and the fathers and chiefly as being "of whom as concerning the flesh Christ came."

Since the question would arise how could God's promises to Israel be reconciled with her present rebellion, Paul answers this. He says, "Not as though the word of God hath taken none effect. For they are not all Israel, which are of Israel." He is simply saying that a Jew is not saved because he is born into Israel and is of the physical seed of Abraham. Just because someone is born into Israel or converts to Judaism doesn't mean he automatically inherits the promises of God. The promises of God are not through the law of Moses.

Paul proves this by pointing out that not all of Abraham's children inherited his promises (Ro. 9:6-8). This is what Paul had already stated in Romans 2:28-29.

John the Baptist and Christ taught the same thing. See Luke 3:8-9; John 8:39-44.

In this passage, Paul uses the term "Israel" in two ways. First, he uses it to refer to all Jews and to all the nation Israel (Ro. 9:4). Then he uses it to refer to the true Israel which is the saved Israel (Ro. 9:6).

Again, Romans 9:6 does not say that a Jew is not a Jew or that an Israelite is not an Israelite. It is not saying that the true Israel consists of New Testament Christians. Paul says nothing here about the church replacing Israel. He is simply explaining what a true Israelite or Jew is before God. He is saying that salvation is not by being a physical descendant of Abraham.

Romans 11:16-24 - For if the firstfruit *be* holy, the lump *is* also *holy*: and if the root *be* holy, so *are* the branches. And if some of the branches be broken off, and thou, being a wild olive tree, wert graffed in among them, and with them partakest of the root and fatness of the olive tree; Boast not against the branches. But if thou boast, thou bearest not the root, but the root thee. Thou wilt say then, The branches were broken off, that I might be graffed in. Well; because of unbelief they were broken off, and thou standest by faith. Be not highminded, but fear: For if God

spared not the natural branches, *take heed* lest he also spare not thee. Behold therefore the goodness and severity of God: on them which fell, severity; but toward thee, goodness, if thou continue in *his* goodness: otherwise thou also shalt be cut off. And they also, if they abide not still in unbelief, shall be graffed in: for God is able to graff them in again. For if thou wert cut out of the olive tree which is wild by nature, and wert graffed contrary to nature into a good olive tree: how much more shall these, which be the natural *branches*, be graffed into their own olive tree?"

This passage is used by those who hold to Replacement Theology to teach that the church and Israel are one tree.

But the context of Romans 11 itself plainly teaches that the church is not Israel and that Israel has a future in God's plan and that her Old Testament covenants will be fulfilled.

Verse 15 says that as there is a casting away of Israel, which is what we see in the current dispensation, so there will be a receiving of Israel which will be associated with the resurrection of the dead (Ro. 11:15). Daniel also associates the restoration of Israel with the resurrection (Da. 12:1-2).

What we see in verses 16-24 is that the church, though different from Israel, is closely associated with spiritual Israel (Ro. 11:16-24). The root is not Israel herself. The root is Abraham's covenant and Abraham's Seed Jesus Christ. Both the church and Israel are connected with this root. There is one tree but different branches. An Old Testament saint like Samuel and a New Testament saint like Apollos are both children of Abraham. Some of the natural branches growing from the root were broken off because of unbelief, and when they repent they will be grafted back in. The natural branches refer to Israel by nature; the Jews are by nature the children of Abraham, but the natural cannot inherit the spiritual kingdom of God.

When Paul warns that professing Christians, too, should fear lest they be found to be in unbelief (Ro. 11:20-21), this is the same type of warning as in Hebrews 3:12 - 4:3. It is a warning about professing Christ without possessing Christ through saving faith.

In verses 25-27, Paul summarizes the issue of the church and Israel in a simple and clear manner. Israel is in spiritual blindness today, and that is what we see in modern Israel, but God isn't finished with blind Israel. She will be saved and converted, and God's covenants with her will be fulfilled. Words could not be plainer. When Paul says that "all Israel shall be saved," he is referring to Israel as a whole Israel and not to every Israelite. This is clear in comparing Scripture with Scripture. All Israel will be saved in the sense of the 12 tribes. Ezekiel tells us that God will restore Judah and Israel and they will be one (Eze. 37:15-20). But Zechariah tells us that only one-third of individual Israelites living in that day will be converted (Zec. 13:8-9). Elsewhere, Paul stated that a remnant of Israel will be saved (Ro. 9:27).

Galatians 3:16 - "Now to Abraham and his seed were the promises made. He saith not, And to seeds, as of many; but as of one, And to thy seed, which is Christ."

Paul taught that Abraham's covenant is fulfilled in and by Christ. He is the promised Seed. He inherits the promises and distributes the blessings.

But Paul nowhere says that Jacob's seed, the 12 tribes of Israel, have ceased to be the seed of Abraham. In the context, he is contrasting the covenant of Abraham with the covenant of Moses. He is proving that the law of Moses was temporary, and the blessing of Abraham and the salvation of God does not come through the law of Moses. It comes through Jesus Christ. See verse 17 - "And this I say, that the covenant, that was confirmed before of God in Christ, the law, which was four hundred and thirty years after, cannot disannul, that it should make the promise of none effect."

Galatians 3:26-29 - "For ye are all the children of God by faith in Christ Jesus. For as many of you as have been baptized into Christ have put on Christ. There is neither

Jew nor Greek, there is neither bond nor free, there is neither male nor female: for ye are all one in Christ Jesus. And if ye be Christ's, then are ye Abraham's seed, and heirs according to the promise."

This passage is speaking about Christ and those who are in Christ. In Christ there is neither Jew nor Greek. All are saved the same way and all become part of the same body today.

But this passage does not say that there is no Jew or Greek today. There are still Jews and Greeks in the flesh, and they must be saved in the same way through faith in Jesus Christ. Paul made this clear elsewhere, when he said that the gospel was to be preached to "the Jew first, and also to the Greek" (Ro. 1:16) and when he divided men into three major groups: Jew, Gentile, and the church of God (1 Co. 10:32).

(Israel is also addressed as Israel multiple times in the book of Acts--Ac. 3:12; 4:8; 5:21, 35; 21:28).

New Testament believers are the seed of Abraham in Christ (Gal. 3:7). They are the children of God. But they are not the nation Israel and they have not replaced the nation Israel, and God is not finished with the nation Israel. New Testament believers are the seed of Abraham, but they are not the seed of Jacob! It is Jacob's seed that will be restored to the land of Israel. See Amos 9:8; Obadiah 1:17; Micah 2:12; 5:8.

Galatians 4:21-26 - "Tell me, ye that desire to be under the law, do ye not hear the law? For it is written, that Abraham had two sons, the one by a bondmaid, the other by a freewoman. But he *who was* of the bondwoman was born after the flesh; but he of the freewoman *was* by promise. Which things are an allegory: for these are the two covenants; the one from the mount Sinai, which gendereth to bondage, which is Agar. For this Agar is mount Sinai in Arabia, and answereth to Jerusalem which now is, and is in bondage with her children. But Jerusalem which is above is free, which is the mother of us all."

The allegory of Galatians 4 cannot support the allegorical interpretation of prophecy, because Paul never interpreted Bible prophecy allegorically, always literally. He described a literal tribulation (1 Th. 5:1-3), a literal Antichrist (2 Th. 2:8-12), a literal resurrection (1 Co. 15), a literal return of Christ with his saints (1 Th. 3:13; 4:14), a literal kingdom to come (2 Ti. 4:1), a literal fulfillment of national Israel's promises (Ro. 11:25-27).

Paul's allegory is different from the allegorical method of interpreting prophecy, because in Galatians 4 Paul assumes the literal existence of Hagar, Sarah, Mount Sinai, Jerusalem, etc. He cites them as allegories only for the purpose of illustration. Those who interpret prophecy allegorically, though, say that Zion is not Zion and that the 144,000 in Revelation 7 is not 144,000 and that the 1,000 years in Revelation chapter 20 is not 1,000 years. This is not what Paul was doing in Galatians 4.

Paul is contrasting the law of Moses with the gospel of saving grace, as he does throughout Galatians. He is refuting the Galatian legalizers who were preaching a works gospel.

Galatians 6:15-16 - "For in Christ Jesus neither circumcision availeth any thing, nor uncircumcision, but a new creature. And as many as walk according to this rule, peace *be* on them, and mercy, and upon the Israel of God."

Those who believe in salvation by grace through Christ Jesus are the ones who are accepted by God and are the true Israel. Paul is saying here the same thing as he said in Romans 2:28-29 and 9:6.

This is not to say that an unsaved Jew is not a Jew or that unsaved Israel today is not Israel or that the church is Israel. Only by isolating Scripture and proof texting and spiritualizing that which can only be literal can one come to such conclusions. By comparing Scripture with Scripture, we know that national Israel has a future in God's program and that her covenants will be literally fulfilled when she submits to Christ.

Paul is using the term "Israel" in a different and broader way than he usually does, but elsewhere he plainly says that Israel is Israel and Jews are Jews. He taught that a remnant of Israel will be saved (Ro. 9:27) and that God's covenants with her will be fulfilled (Ro. 11:25-27).

"All the 65 other occurrences of the term 'Israel' in the New Testament refer to Jews" (*Bible Knowledge Commentary*).

Ephesians 1:10 - "That in the dispensation of the fulness of times he might gather together in one all things in Christ, both which are in heaven, and which are on earth; *even* in him."

God's great plan for the ages is to make Christ the Head of a new creation. Everything will be gathered together in Christ. The Bible is the revelation of this plan. The completion of this program is seen in the last two chapters of the book of Revelation. The old heaven and earth will be burned up (as per 2 Peter 3) and there will be a new heaven and a new earth, and the citizens of this new universe will dwell in the New Jerusalem and on the new earth. Christ, God manifest in the flesh, will be the Head of this new universe and every man and every creature will be properly related to and centered in Christ as Head.

But what Paul describes in Ephesians 1:10 does not address the issue of Israel and the church. Paul does not say here that Israel and the church are the same. He only says that ultimately everything will be one in Christ. To say that is not to say that there aren't different groups of saved people in Christ.

One must go to other Scriptures to answer such questions, and other Scriptures are clear that the nation Israel is not the same as the church and that God's covenants with the nation Israel are inherited by the church. The saved of Israel and the saved of the church age are all saved by the blood of Christ and are all one in Him spiritually, but there remain distinctions.

Ephesians 2:13-16 - "But now in Christ Jesus ye who sometimes were far off are made nigh by the blood of Christ. For he is our peace, who hath made both one, and hath broken down the middle wall of partition between us; Having abolished in his flesh the enmity, even the law of commandments contained in ordinances; for to make in himself of twain one new man, so making peace; And that he might reconcile both unto God in one body by the cross, having slain the enmity thereby."

Replacement Theology says that this passage teaches that Israel and the church are one body, one new man, that the church has been added to the body of Israel.

> "In the inspired writings of Paul, he clearly teaches that God is taking two peoples and making them into one people" (Matt Furse, *Who Is Israel?*).

But Paul is not teaching here that Israel and the church are one body. He is teaching that Jews and Gentiles are one new body, which is the church. The church is the body and the new man.

Paul does not say here that Israel is the church and Israel's covenants are fulfilled in the church.

To say that Jews and Gentiles are brought together into a new body, the church, conforms to the Bible's consistent teaching that God is not finished with Israel *as* 12 tribes of Israel and that her covenants will yet be fulfilled literally on earth.

But to say that Israel and the church are the body and the new man of Ephesians throws the Bible into confusion and forces the interpreter to allegorize massive amounts of Scripture that are clearly intended to be literal.

(By the way, in dealing with the teaching of Ephesians 2-3, Pastor Furse mistakenly says that Dispensational Theology makes an error by saying that the church age comes to an end. He says, "Dispensationalism teaches that there is a 'church age' that comes to an end, however, the inspired

Word of God teaches that there will be 'glory in the church by Christ Jesus throughout all ages, world without end' (Ephesians 3:21)" (*Who Is the Church?*). But to say that the church *age* has an end is not to say that the church itself has an end. I have never read anywhere that a Dispensationalist has said the church has an end.)

Ephesians 2:19-22 - "Now therefore ye are no more strangers and foreigners, but fellowcitizens with the saints, and of the household of God; And are built upon the foundation of the apostles and prophets, Jesus Christ himself being the chief corner *stone*; In whom all the building fitly framed together groweth unto an holy temple in the Lord: In whom ye also are builded together for an habitation of God through the Spirit."

Those who hold to Replacement Theology claim that here Paul is teaching that the church is one with redeemed Israel as one building and one temple.

But the Bible teaches as plainly as it says anything that Israel will be saved and her earthly covenants will be fulfilled. Paul himself says this in Romans 11:25-27.

So on the one hand, the Bible says that Israel has a future in God's prophetic program and her Old Testament covenants will be literally fulfilled, and on the other hand the Bible says that the church is a mystery body not seen by Old Testament prophets and that the church is already seated in heavenly places (Eph. 2:6).

The question is, what relationship does restored, converted Israel have with the church?

In what sense is there one building and one temple?

The answer is that there is one building, but there are different aspects of the building, different parts of the building, different rooms, so to speak. Paul is dealing with metaphors which teach spiritual truths, but in Ephesians 2 he is not stating everything that can be said about the church and Israel. He is making one major point, and that is that

God's eternal plan is for everything to be one in Christ as a habitation of God (Eph. 2:22). This was God's plan for man from the beginning. Man was made for God. Man is to love God with all his heart, soul, and strength (De. 6:5). That is man's chief purpose. God made the creation for man to enjoy (1 Ti. 6:17), but man's passion is to be directed to the lovely Creator Himself. This was lost in the fall, when man began to worship and serve the creature more than the Creator (Ro. 1:25), but man's proper relationship with his Creator will be restored and taken to a much higher level in the new creation, and the church is the firstfruits of the new creation (Jas. 1:18). The church is one part of the new creation. Converted and restored Israel will be another part of the new creation.

Paul says in Ephesians 2 that there one holy temple in the Lord (Eph. 2:21), spiritually, but we know that there will be a literal millennial temple on earth in Jerusalem, and it is associated with Israel. It will have Levitical priests (Eze. 44:15-31) and sacrifices (Eze. 46:1-6). This is not the church, but we also know that church age saints will be ruling and reigning with Christ at that same time (Re. 2:26-27).

Personally, I don't believe that the Bible reveals exactly how redeemed Israel and the church relate to one another in the one spiritual temple of God (as per Ephesians 2) and as part of the one spiritual tree growing from the one root, which is Christ (as per Romans 11:26-24). There are many questions that are not yet answered on these matters.

Philippians 3:3 - "For we are the circumcision, which worship God in the spirit, and rejoice in Christ Jesus, and have no confidence in the flesh."

In this verse, Paul is saying that born again New Testament saints are the true circumcision, meaning they fulfill the true spiritual meaning of circumcision, which points to the circumcision of the heart, to knowing and loving God from the heart, to a rejection of self-righteousness for the true righteousness in Christ, rather than mere external ritual and confidence in religion and ritual.

The verse does not say that New Testament believers have become the true Israel and replaced Israel. It doesn't say that God's covenants with Israel are fulfilled in the church.

Hebrews 12:22-23 - "But ye are come unto mount Sion, and unto the city of the living God, the heavenly Jerusalem, and to an innumerable company of angels, To the general assembly and church of the firstborn, which are written in heaven, and to God the Judge of all, and to the spirits of just men made perfect.

This passage contrasts the law of Moses with the gospel of salvation by the grace of God in Christ. See Hebrews 12:18-24.

The passage actually supports the doctrine that the church is not Israel by teaching that the church's portion and hope is heavenly. The New Testament believer is seated in heavenly places in Christ positionally (Eph. 2:6). Therefore it is said that we are come unto the heavenly Jerusalem. We are exhorted to set our affections there rather than on this earth (Col. 3:1-4).

The passage says nothing about national Israel and her covenants. The author of Hebrews does not say that God is finished with Israel and that her covenants are fulfilled in the church. The passage does not and cannot negate all of the clear teaching of Scripture on a literal fulfillment of the Return Covenant (De. 29-30), the Davidic Covenant (2 Samuel 7), and the New Covenant (Je. 31-33).

The present earthly Jerusalem points both to the heavenly Jerusalem and to the glorified Jerusalem that will be the headquarters of the Messianic kingdom.

Jesus is said to be "the mediator of the new covenant," but this does not mean that the New Covenant is fulfilled in the church and has no literal fulfillment in Israel. As Hebrews teaches in chapters 8 and 10, the New Covenant has elements that extend beyond Israel and her conversion and restoration and glorification. *New Testament believers participate in the spiritual blessings of the New Covenant* through Christ's atonement. We see this in He. 8:8-11 (quoting from Jer. 31:31-34), where the writer cites only the spiritual aspects of the New Covenant. We see this in He. 10:15-18, where the writer again refers only the spiritual aspects of the New Covenant. Nowhere does Hebrews or any other New Testament epistle say that this covenant has been *transferred* from national Israel to "the church" or that the physical aspects of the covenant should be spiritualized.

The writer of Hebrews does not quote from the New Covenant to teach that the "church" rather than Israel has inherited it, but rather to show that the Old Testament itself pointed to a time when the Mosaic sacrifices would no longer be made (He. 10:16-18).

Revelation 3:9 - "Behold, I will make them of the synagogue of Satan, which say they are Jews, and are not, but do lie; behold, I will make them to come and worship before thy feet, and to know that I have loved thee."

Here Jesus is condemning the self-righteous religion of Judaism that hated and rejected the gospel and persecuted New Testament Christians. They boasted themselves as the true Jews and the true people of God, but they were deceived. The Lord Jesus says that they will come and worship before the feet of Christians and will know that God loves them and is pleased with them.

This verse says nothing about Christians being the true Israel or replacing Israel or inheriting Israel's covenants.

Revelation 21:10-14 - "And he carried me away in the spirit to a great and high mountain, and shewed me that great city, the holy Jerusalem, descending out of heaven from God, Having the glory of God: and her light *was* like unto a stone most precious, even like a jasper stone, clear as crystal; And had a wall great and high, *and* had twelve

110

gates, and at the gates twelve angels, and names written thereon, which are *the names* of the twelve tribes of the children of Israel: On the east three gates; on the north three gates; on the south three gates; and on the west three gates. And the wall of the city had twelve foundations, and in them the names of the twelve apostles of the Lamb."

Here we see that even in the new heaven and new earth there will remain a distinction between Israel and the church. They will live in the same New Jerusalem. They will be one in Christ. They will have one Head, which is Christ. But there will still be the 12 tribes of Israel and the 12 apostles of the church.

God doesn't tell us exactly how they will be different at that time. It is not for us to worry about. We have enough revelation to know that God's covenants with national Israel in Deuteronomy 29-20 and Jeremiah 31-33, etc., will yet be fulfilled in national Israel and not in the church. We don't allegorize or spiritualize those great covenant prophecies so that they become nearly meaningless. We interpret them literally and let the words of God say what they say in a normal-literal manner, and by that means we know that Israel and the church are not the same, and that God is not finished with national Israel.

Christ Is Israel

Covenant theologians site prophecies that identify Christ as Israel and come to the *wrong* conclusion that Israel as a nation has no future beyond her current apostasy and that her covenants are fulfilled rather in the church.

Consider Isaiah 49:

"Listen, O isles, unto me; and hearken, ye people, from far; The LORD hath called me from the womb; from the bowels of my mother hath he made mention of my name. And he hath made my mouth like a sharp sword; in the shadow of his hand hath he hid me, and made me a polished shaft; in

111

his quiver hath he hid me; And said unto me, Thou art my servant, O Israel, in whom I will be glorified" (Isaiah 49:1-3).

Isaiah 49-53 is the longest and most beautiful Messianic prophecy in the Old Testament Scripture. It teaches that the Messiah is God's Instrument of redemption, not only to redeem Israel, but also to redeem the entire world. Ultimately, everything will be one in Christ in a new heaven and new earth. That is God's great plan of the ages.

In Isaiah 49:3, Christ is called Israel. "Israel" means "who prevails with God" (Ge. 32:28), but here "Israel" does not refer to Jacob; it refers to the greater Israel, who is Christ. Only in Christ is Jacob Israel, just as only in Christ is the New Testament believer a saint. We are "accepted in the beloved" (Eph. 1:6). The Father accepts the Son and His sacrifice, and the believing creation is accepted in the Son.

That Christ is Israel is an important and powerful and wonderful teaching, but it cannot be made to say, though, that the nation Israel is no longer Israel today and that Israel's national covenants have ceased to have a future in a national Israel and that the church is Israel in the sense that national Israel is not any longer Israel. Those conclusions are contrary to the clear teaching of the whole Bible, as we have seen.

Cursing and Imprecatory Prayers

In August 2009, Steven Anderson said in a sermon "Why I Hate Barack Obama" that he prayed for the death of U.S. President Barack Obama. He told Michaelangelo Signorile that he "would not judge or condemn" anyone who killed the president (Evelyn Schlatter, "18 Anti-Gay Groups and Their Propaganda," SPLC).

That is not New Testament Christianity. It is cultic weirdness.

Where in the New Testament do we see the apostles and early Christians acting like this in reference to the Roman emperor?

When James and John wanted to call down fire from heaven on the Samaritans, Christ "rebuked them, and said, Ye know not what manner of spirit ye are of. For the Son of man is not come to destroy men's lives, but to save them..." (Luke 9:55).

When listening to Steven Anderson's preaching, I have often wondered what spirit he is of.

Cursing homosexuals

In 2014, Anderson preached,

> "Here's what the Bible says, Leviticus 20:13, 'If a man also lie with mankind, as he lieth with a woman, both of them have committed an abomination. They shall surely be put to death. Their blood shall be upon them.' And that, my friend, is the cure for AIDS. It was right there in the Bible all along. Because if you executed the homos, like God recommends, you wouldn't have all this AIDS running rampant" ("Pastor Calls for Killing Gays," *USA Today*, Dec. 6, 2014).

> "I do hate homosexuals and if hating homosexuals makes our church a hate group then that's what we are" (cited from Schlatter, SPLC).

Of the 2016 Orlando nightclub shooting Anderson said, "The good news is that there's 50 less pedophiles in this world, because these homosexuals are just a bunch of disgusting perverts and pedophiles" ("Gay Hating Preacher," *Sunday Express*, Sept. 16, 2016).

Anderson said it was too bad some of the homosexuals survived.

As we saw earlier, Pastor Roger Jimenez, Verity Baptist Church, Sacramento, California, who appears in Anderson's video *Marching to Zion*, repeated Anderson's statement about the Orlando shooting almost word for word in his own pulpit. He said, "The tragedy is more of them didn't die. ... I'm kind of upset he didn't finish the job."

Of transgender celebrity Bruce (Caitlyn) Jenner, Anderson said in a sermon,

> "Listen to me – I hate him with a perfect hatred. I have no love for this Bruce freak. I hope he dies today, I hope he dies and goes to Hell – he's disgusting, he's filthy, he's reprobate. You evil, filthy animal that's destroying the morals of our country – die. ... I hate these filthy sons of Belial – they're disgusting and sick. That guy will never find Jesus – the Bible says he's reprobate, the Bible explains why people would lust after another man when you're a man. ... I hope God touches Bruce Jenner's heart like this [referring to the movie Indiana Jones and the Temple of Doom where the priest pulls a man's still-beating heart from his chest] I pray that his heart would explode right now. ... Nobody who defends that freak is welcome in this church! ... This person is just the evangelist of sodomy and filth to the world, and people are like, 'Oh, we need to pray for him so that he finds Jesus.' I'm going to pray that he dies and goes to Hell" (Adam Salandra, "Pastor Prays Caitlyn Jenner's Heart Explodes," NewNowNex, n.d.).

Anderson's statement about Jenner can be found in the following series of sermon excerpts:
www.youtube.com/watch?v=ttxumEkHnKE

In September 2016, Anderson was banned from the U.K., South Africa, and Botswana. He was subsequently banned from Malawi.

Anderson teaches that there is no hope for homosexuals to be saved. He believes homosexuals are beyond the scope of God's eternal mercy. On his video, "Born That Way?" he says,

> "... once people die and go to hell it's too late for them. Well, I'm just saying that the Bible teaches in many places that it can become too late for a person before that point sometimes, if they reject Christ enough. And I would say homosexuals fall into that category" (about 7:07f).

In his paper and video "The Truth about Homosexuals," he cites Romans 1 and says, "God has already rejected the sodomites."

Anderson preaches that no homosexuals are welcome in his church.

> "There are no queers allowed in this church. No homos will ever be allowed in this church as long as I am the pastor here. Never!"
>
> www.youtube.com/watch?v=ttxumEkHnKE

In reply to Anderson's position we would make the following points:"

1. The law of Moses did pronounce a death sentence upon homosexuality, *as well as upon* adultery, fornication, stealing, kidnapping, sabbath breaking, blasphemy, idolatry, and other sins.

2. We do not live under the law of Moses. That law was given to Israel to prepare for the coming of Christ, to show men that God is a holy judge and that we are condemned sinners, and to lead men to salvation in Christ. See Romans 3:19-24; Galatians 3:10-14, 24.

3. We do not live in a theocracy. The Protestants who established city states and placed the citizens under the law of Moses, such as the city state that John Calvin set up in Geneva, were unscriptural churches. The Protestant churches

in the early history of America that put witches to death were unscriptural churches. One of the fundamental errors was the very "replacement theology" that Steven Anderson has adopted.

4. In His mercy, God is in the saving business today. This is the age of worldwide gospel preaching. Jesus was born under the law of Moses that He might fulfill the requirements of the law in the place of sinners. He came to seek and to save that which was lost (Luke 19:10). The Good News is that the Son of God died for the sins of the world and that eternal salvation is available by repentance and faith. This is the gospel that is to be preached to *every person* in every nation in this age (Mark 16:15; Acts 1:8). Why would Christ command that the gospel be preached to every creature if He did not intend to save every creature? The Bible answers that by telling us that God does indeed want all sinners to be saved (1 Timothy 2:3-6). There are no exceptions. "But the scripture hath concluded all under sin, that the promise by faith of Jesus Christ might be given to them that believe" (Ga. 3:22).

5. When James and John wanted to call down fire upon those who rejected Christ, He rebuked them and said they were of the wrong spirit (Luke 9:54-56).

6. Romans 1:32 does say that homosexuals are "worthy of death." They are worthy of death in God's sight and will suffer eternal death if they do not repent. But the same verse applies to every sin mentioned in the passage, including covetousness, envy, debate, deceit, malignity, whisperers, backbiters, proud, spiteful, disobedient to parents, without understanding, covenant breakers, without natural affection, implacable, unmerciful (Romans 1:29-31). Romans 1:32 can't be applied only to homosexuality. Further, Scripture must be interpreted in context. In this passage Paul is not addressing the issue of what should or should not be a crime under secular government in this age, nor is he addressing the issue of capital punishment under secular government. He is

addressing the issue of man's fall, and he is proving that all men are sinners and are therefore guilty before God of death and that salvation is available in Christ. This is the clear theme of Romans 1-3. Paul is teaching that *every one of those sins* will be visited with eternal death if the practitioners do not repent and trust Christ, but that *every one of those sins* are forgiven in Christ.

7. Homosexuality is no light matter. It is a corruption of God's natural creation, an abomination before God, and a poisonous thing in society. In Romans 1, Paul describes it as "vile affections" (v. 26), "against nature" (v. 26), "unseemly" (v. 27), and "a reprobate mind" (v. 28). The rapid spread of homosexuality and its broad acceptance in our day is a sign of end time apostasy. Christ mentions "Sodom" in connection with His return (Lu. 17:29-30).

8. *Any* sinner should be welcome to attend church services as visitors, so long as they don't cause trouble, because the church's goal is to invite all people to God's salvation. On any given week we have adulterers, fornicators, homosexuals, polygamists, idolaters, thieves, liars, and demon possessed people in our church services. Anyone is welcome to attend the services to hear the preaching of God's Word. On the other hand, church membership requires salvation and evidence of the new birth. This is what we see in the early churches. The membership of the church of Corinth is described as follows:

> "Know ye not that the unrighteous shall not inherit the kingdom of God? Be not deceived: neither fornicators, nor idolaters, nor adulterers, nor effeminate, nor abusers of themselves with mankind, Nor thieves, nor covetous, nor drunkards, nor revilers, nor extortioners, shall inherit the kingdom of God. And SUCH WERE SOME OF YOU: but ye are washed, but ye are sanctified, but ye are justified in the name of the Lord Jesus, and by the Spirit of our God" (1 Corinthians 6:9-11).

The membership of the early churches was composed of sinners of all types who had been forgiven and converted by the power of God so that they were new creatures in Christ. They weren't sinless, but they were on a new path and had a new life and walked according to a new rule.

In 1 Corinthians 6 we see that homosexuals *can* be saved and experience a changed life in Jesus Christ, and they are saved in the same way as any other sinner: by repenting of their sin against God and surrendering to His authority and believing on Jesus Christ as Saviour with all the heart.

> "Testifying both to the Jews, and also to the Greeks, repentance toward God, and faith toward our Lord Jesus Christ" (Acts 20:21).

Christ Suffered in Hell

Steven Anderson has latched onto another heresy, and this one is fundamental. He says that Christ paid for man's sins by suffering in hell for three days and three nights."

> "Not only did His body die, but His soul went to hell. That is death" (Steven Anderson, "Jesus Went to Hell to Pay for Our Sins").

> "What's the significance of the Passover being roasted with fire? It says that Jesus Christ went to hell for three days and three nights" ("Jesus Went to Hell").

> "Speaking of how that hell is an eternal place, Jesus suffered an eternity of hell in those three days and three nights, if you think about what this verse is saying in Jonah 2" ("Jesus Went to Hell").

> "People will say that on the cross everything was done. 'It is finished.' But it is not true. What it really is is that Jesus went to hell and suffered the wrath of God for our sins" ("Jesus Went to Hell").

> "I believe that Jesus Christ's soul was in a place of torment for three days and three nights" (Anderson interview with James White).

1. This heresy is based on a misinterpretation of the word "hell" in the Old Testament.

Anderson uses the following passages as proof texts for his doctrine:

> "For thou wilt not leave my soul in HELL; neither wilt thou suffer thine Holy One to see corruption" (Ps. 16:10). This verse is cited in Acts 2:27

> "And said, I cried by reason of mine affliction unto the LORD, and he heard me; out of the belly of HELL cried I, and thou heardest my voice" (Jon. 2:2).

The word "hell" in these passages is translated from the Hebrew "sheol," which has two meanings. Sometimes "sheol" means the place where the bodies of the dead are laid (Ps. 6:5; Ec. 9:10; Isa.38:18, 19). Usually, "sheol" refers to the place where departed spirits go (Ge. 37:35; De. 32:22; Ps. 9:17; 55:15; 30:3; Pr. 9:18; 15:24; 23:14; Isa. 5:14; 14:15; Eze. 31:16; 32:21, 27).

In the New Testament, "sheol" is translated by the Greek word "hades." This is the word used in Acts 2:27, when Peter quotes from Psalm 16:10. Thus the "sheol" of the Old Testament is the "hades" of the New.

That it had two compartments seems apparent from the fact that both the saved (David in Ps. 16:10) and the unsaved (all nations that forget God in Ps. 9:17) went to "sheol."

It appears that Christ described this in the account of the rich man and Lazarus in Luke 16:23. That this is not a parable is obvious in that Christ did not call it a parable and in that He named the names of Abraham and Lazarus, something He never did in His parables. This is not a parable. It is an account of two men who died and went into eternity. The unsaved man went to *hades* and the saved man went to *Abraham's bosom*. From *hades*, the rich man talked to Abraham who told him that there was an impassable gulf between the two places. These are probably the two parts or compartments in *sheol* or *hades*.

Christ did not go to the place of torment. He went rather to paradise, as He promised the repentant thief on the cross, "Today shalt thou be with me in paradise" (Lu. 23:43). This probably refers to Abraham's bosom. Matthew 12:40 says Christ went into "the heart of the earth." This is what Paul is referring to in Ephesians 4:9, which says that Christ descended "into the lower parts of the earth." Apparently this is the location of *sheol* or *hades*.

When Christ rose from the dead, He announced His victory to the unsaved (1 Pe. 3:18-20), and He took the saved to heaven as trophies of His victory (Eph. 4:8-9). He emptied

Abraham's bosom. It is like a victorious king who rescues the captives and brings the captives and the loot on his victory parade. We see examples of this in Ge. 14:14-16 and 1 Sa. 30:3-34.

2. One thing is clear, and that is that Christ did not go to a burning hell for three days and nights to suffer for man's sins.

Christ paid the atonement for sin on the cross itself by His death and blood (Ro. 5:8-9). The Levitical sacrifices teach us that it is *the blood* that makes the atonement (Le. 17:11; He. 9:22). We are redeemed by Christ's precious blood (1 Pe. 1:19).

It was on the cross itself where Christ was made sin for us (2 Co. 5:21). It was then that the holy Father turned away from Him and Christ cried, "My God, my God, why hast thou forsaken me?" (Mt. 27:46).

Just before Christ died, He announced, "It is finished" (Joh. 19:30). And the veil in the temple was rent, signifying that the way to God was open through Christ's atonement (Mr. 15:38). There was no atoning price left to pay in "hell."

Denying the Imminency of the Rapture

Steven Anderson has produced a number of presentations denying the imminency of the Rapture, chiefly a video series entitled *The Book of Revelation* and the slickly produced movie *After the Tribulation*.

In *After the Tribulation*, Anderson is joined by Kent Hovind who has recently changed his position on prophecy and has adopted what he calls the "post-trib, pre-wrath position."

Anderson calls the Pre-Tribulation Rapture "a demonic deception," a "lie," a "fraud," a "fairy tale."

(Emerging church leaders use similar terminology to demonize the doctrine of an imminent Rapture, as we have documented in the report "Hating the Rapture" at www.wayoflife.org.)

Anderson says, "The film [*After the Tribulation*] does two major things—number one, it completely demolishes the fraud that is the Pre-Trib Rapture. You know, this lie that says that Jesus Christ can come back at any moment, and that we're going to be taken out of here before the Antichrist, before the global government. So about half the movie is spent just completely destroying that idea; just a ton of Scripture is used to prove that false. And then the other half of the movie pretty much just explains how all this is going to play out..." (*The Alex Jones Nightly News*, Feb. 1, 2013).

Anderson's presentations on prophecy do indeed include "a ton of Scripture," but a ton of Scripture wrongly interpreted adds up to no Scripture at all.

In "After the Tribulation," he teaches that the Rapture will occur *after* the Tribulation, but in part 2 of the video series "The Book of Revelation," he says that the Rapture will happen 75 days after the "abomination of desolation," which occurs at the mid-point of the Antichrist's seven-year covenant with Israel. And in part 15 he says the Rapture will occur after the tribulation but before God's wrath is poured out.

The bottom line is that the Rapture cannot be imminent, and he plainly states this. Anderson says, "The Rapture simply cannot happen at any moment" (*After the Tribulation*, 01:27:05).

If Anderson is right, it would be a matter of waiting until we see the Antichrist arise and make his covenant with Israel and rebuild the Jewish temple, and waiting until we observe the Two Witnesses preaching and being killed and rising from the dead, and waiting until we see the Antichrist desecrate the temple, which is "the abomination of desolation," and exactly 75 days later the Rapture will occur. We would, therefore, be able to set the exact day of the Rapture.

The Bible's Description of the Rapture

The word "Rapture" does not appear in Scripture, but the event is plainly described in 1 Thessalonians 4:13 - 5:11 and 1 Corinthians 15:51-58. The Greek word translated "caught up" in 1 Thessalonians 4:17 is used in Acts 8:39 of the Spirit of God snatching away Philip after the conversion of the Ethiopian eunuch.

1 Thessalonians 4:13 - 5:11

This is the most extensive passage in the Bible on the Rapture.

Some of the lessons are as follows:

1. The Rapture is an event in which the dead in Christ will be raised (1 Th. 4:14-16) and the living New Testament saints will be changed and glorified (1 Th. 4:17).

2. The dead in Christ are presently with Him in heaven (1 Th. 4:14). The dead in Christ do not "sleep in the grave" as some false teachers claim.

3. The Rapture is the believer's hope and comfort (1 Th. 4:13, 18). This is what we are waiting for. We are looking for Christ, not the Antichrist. This is the believer's "blessed hope" (Titus 2:13).

4. The Rapture occurs before the Day of the Lord's wrath (1 Th. 5:1-10).

   a. The "Day of the Lord" is the time of Tribulation when God will judge the world for its sin and idolatry. In that "day," God will be exalted and rebellious men will be humbled. See Isaiah 2:10-21.

   b. Note the change in pronouns in 1 Thessalonians 5:1-10. In verse 3 the pronoun "they" is used, because the Day of the Lord will come upon the unsaved world. But in verses 4-5 the pronoun "ye" is used, referring to believers. That day will not overtake us.

   c. The believer is to be watching for the Lord's return at all times ("let us watch and be sober," 1 Th. 5:6). We do not know when it will happen. It is imminent.

   d. Church age believers are not appointed to go through the time of God's wrath (1 Th. 5:9). Compare 1 Thessalonians 1:10. Believers have been subject to the wrath of men and devils throughout the church age, but we are not appointed to go through the wrath of God that will be poured out upon this wicked world. Compare Isaiah 2:9-21.

   e. The place of spiritual protection during the days of apostasy before the Rapture is the New Testament church (1 Th. 5:12-14). Each believer needs to be a faithful member of a church that is led by godly men who are sound in the New Testament faith. The leaders and the church members work together to accomplish God's will on earth in preaching the gospel to every nation while they wait for the Lord's return. The way to have peace in the church is for the leaders to teach the Bible faithfully and for the members to show respect to the leaders and follow them as they follow Christ and His Word. Those who are unruly in the churches should be rebuked, because they harm the Lord's work.

1 Corinthians 15:51-58

1. The Rapture is a mystery that was not revealed in Old Testament prophecy (1 Co. 15:51). The Old Testament prophets taught about the bodily resurrection, but they did not teach that some would be glorified without dying. They prophesied about the resurrection of Jews at the end of the Tribulation (Da. 12:1-2), but they did not see the Rapture of New Testament believers before the Tribulation.

2. The dead in Christ will be raised to incorruption and the believers who are living at that time will be instantly changed from mortal to immortal (1 Co. 15:52-53). "Incorruptible" means that the resurrection body will be incapable of such things as pain and sickness. "Immortal" means incapable of dying.

3. The Rapture of church-age believers is to be a source of great encouragement and motivation to godly Christian service (1 Co. 15:58). The imminent Rapture is a very important doctrine. It helps to motivate the Lord's people to stay awake spiritually, and it helps to motivate the churches to stay busy in the work of preaching the gospel to lost souls before it is too late. It helps them not to be sidetracked from this work.

4. What about "the last trump"?

The trumpet that will sound at the Rapture of church-age saints has nothing to do with the trumpets that will sound in Revelation as judgments on this world or the trumpets that sound in reference to Israel. The church is not a part of these other programs. Her "trump" is a different one. The church's last trump is when she shall be congregated together to the Lord (1 Th. 4:17).

Why We Hold to a Pre-Trib Rapture

There are some difficulties with any position on the timing of the Rapture and some questions that cannot be answered with certainty, but having studied this matter from all sides for four and a half decades, following are three of the fundamental Bible truths that convince me that the Rapture is Pre-Tribulation.

1. The Rapture of church-age saints is said to be imminent (it could happen any time), whereas the Second Coming is said to be preceded by specific signs.

Christ taught that the Rapture is imminent (Matthew 24:42, 44; 25:13; Mark 13:32-37).

Paul taught that the Rapture is imminent (Php. 4:5; Tit. 2:12-13).

James taught that the Rapture is imminent (Jas. 5:8-9).

Peter taught that the Rapture is imminent (1 Pe. 4:7).

The early Christians were living in constant expectation of Christ's return ("to wait for his Son from heaven," 1 Th. 1:9-10). As we have seen, the apostle Paul instructed the church at Thessalonica that they did not need to heed signs and times, because the New Testament believer has been promised redemption from the "day of darkness" that shall overcome the whole world (1 Th. 5:1-9). The church is waiting for Christ, not the Antichrist.

2. The church is a mystery that is not revealed in the Old Testament (Eph. 3:1-11).

The New Testament church has no part in the chronology of events foretold by the Old Testament prophets. They clearly foretold the first coming of Christ as the Suffering Messiah: His miraculous birth, sinless life, atoning death, bodily resurrection, and ascension. The same prophets describe Christ's Second Coming as the Reigning Messiah, preceded by a time of unprecedented worldwide tribulation and followed by the establishment of the glorious Messianic kingdom centered in Jerusalem. But these prophets did not see the church--"*which in other ages was not made known unto the sons of men, as it is now revealed unto his holy apostles and prophets by the Spirit*" (Eph. 3:5).

Between Christ's first and second coming, there is a time gap that was not seen by the Old Testament prophets. This gap is the church age. The prophets did not see that Israel would be set aside temporarily while God called out from among all nations a special body of people. After He has accomplished this purpose and the fullness of the Gentiles is come in, God will restart Israel's prophetic clock, so to speak, with the last seven years of Daniel's 70th Week (Da. 9:24-28) and will fulfill all Old Testament prophecies and covenants pertaining to His ancient chosen nation. "... *blindness in part is happened to Israel, until the fulness of the Gentiles be come in*" (Ro. 11:25).

The Great Tribulation pertains to God's dealing with Israel and the Gentile nations, not to the church. This present mystery period will end with the removal of church-age believers from the earth; and the Lord will then pour out His judgments on the Gentile nations and fulfill His covenants with Israel. The Great Tribulation is called "the time of the heathen" (Eze. 30:3), referring to the Gentile nations, and "the time of Jacob's trouble" (Jer. 30:7), referring to Israel.

3. The book of Revelation shows that the church is not on earth during the Tribulation.

    a. The church is not seen on earth in chapters 4-18.

    b. The witness for God in the earth during the Tribulation is Israel, not the church (Re. 7).

    c. The prayers of the saints in Revelation 8 are prayers for judgment. Only Israel prayed such prayers. Church-age saints are instructed to pray *for* their enemies, not *against* them (Lu. 9:51-56). The imprecatory prayers of Revelation are those of the

Psalms and are based on God's promise to Abraham to curse those that cursed Israel (Gen. 12:1-3).

d. The scorpion-like creatures of Revelation 9 are given freedom to hurt all earth-dwellers except those Jews who were sealed by the angel of Revelation 7. If church-age believers were on earth, they would be subject to this horrible judgment.

e. Revelation 10 identifies the events of Revelation 4-18 with those foretold by Old Testament prophets--the days of the Great Tribulation, the "Day of the Lord." The church age was never in the view of these Old Testament prophecies. It was a mystery not yet revealed. The church has a different purpose and program than national Israel. It is Israel that is in view in Old Testament prophecy and in Revelation 4-18.

f. The ministry of the two witnesses of Revelation 11 identifies them with national Israel and with Old Testament prophecies of the *"Day of the Lord."* The two witnesses minister from Jerusalem, Israel's capital. The churches have no such capital, her hope being heavenly, not earthly (Col. 3:1-4; Php. 3:17-21). The two witnesses are clothed in sackcloth, which speaks of Israel. The sackcloth signifies repentance from sin and sorrow because of some calamity (1 Ki. 21:27; 2 Ki. 19:1; Est. 4:1; Isa. 15:3; Jer. 4:8). Nowhere are the churches seen in sackcloth. The churches are told, rather, to *"rejoice in the Lord alway"* (Php. 4:4). The church-age believer's judgment is past, and he is to keep his mind centered in the heavenlies where, positionally, he is already seated, victorious with Christ (Eph. 2:5-10). Revelation 11:4 identifies the two witnesses with the Old Testament prophecy of Zechariah 4:3, 11, 14. This is a prophecy about Israel, not the church. Further, the two witnesses call down judgment upon their enemies in Revelation 10:5-6.

Jesus rebuked His disciples for desiring to do just this and instructed the church-age believer to pray for the well-being of his enemies, not for their destruction (Lu. 9:54-56; Ro. 12:14, 17-21).

g. The devil persecutes Israel, not the church, during the Tribulation (Re. 12). There can be no doubt that the woman in this chapter signifies Israel. Verse 5 shows the woman bringing forth Christ; it is obvious that Jesus was brought forth by Israel, not by the churches (Isa. 9:6-7; Ro. 9:5). Also, the symbols of Revelation 12:1-2 recall familiar Old Testament typology of Israel. She is referred to as a woman (Isa. 54:5-7). The sun and moon and the 12 stars of verse 2 remind us of Joseph's dream regarding Israel (Gen. 37:9). The words of Revelation 12:2 are almost an exact quote from Micah 5:3, again speaking of Israel's delivery of the Messiah. These symbols are not used in the New Testament of the churches.

When Was the Pre-Trib Rapture First Taught?

Steven Anderson follows Replacement theologians in claiming that John Darby was the first to teach a Pre-Tribulation Rapture, but it isn't true.

As we have seen, two thousand years ago, all of the churches were looking for an imminent return of Christ. That was a long time before Darby.

In the 4th century, the Pre-Tribulation Rapture was taught by **Ephraem the Syrian** (c. 303-373). Ephraem is called "the Syrian" because he lived in that region.

Ephraem is venerated as a "saint" by the Catholic and Orthodox churches, but they would not allow him to teach his doctrine of prophecy today.

He was a voluminous writer. Many of his sermons and psalms are included in the 16-volume *Post-Nicene Library*. (The Council of Nicea was held in AD 325, and historians divide the "fathers" into Ante-Nicene, before 325, and Post-Nicene, after 325).

In the 1990s some of Ephraem's writings were translated into English for the first time, one of these being *On the Last Times, the Antichrist, and the End of the World*, A.D. 373.

The translation was done by Professor Cameron Rhoades of Tyndale Theological Seminary at the bequest of Grant R. Jeffrey. It was subsequently published in Jeffrey's 1995 book *Final Warning.*

It is obvious that Ephraem believed in a literal fulfillment of prophecy, including a Rapture of New Testament saints prior to the Tribulation.

> **"For all the saints and Elect of God are gathered, prior to the tribulation that is to come, and are taken to the Lord lest they see the confusion that is to overwhelm the world because of our sins"** (Ephraem the Syrian, *On the Last Times*).

Observe that Ephraem taught that the saints will be taken to the Lord so they will not see the confusion that is to overwhelm the world, which is exactly what 1 Thessalonians 5:3-9 says.

Ephraem taught a literal Antichrist who will sit in a literal rebuilt temple in Jerusalem, a literal 3.5 year Tribulation, a literal Two Witnesses or prophets who will preach in Jerusalem, a literal battle of Gog and Magog.

> "And when the three and a half years have been completed, the time of the Antichrist, through which he will have seduced the world, after the resurrection of the two prophets, in the hour which the world does not know, and on the day which the enemy or son of perdition does not know, will come the sign of the Son of Man, and coming forward the Lord shall appear with great power and much majesty, with the sign of the word of salvation going before him, and also even with all the powers of the heavens with the whole chorus of the saints. ... Then Christ shall come and the enemy shall be thrown into confusion, and the Lord shall

131

destroy him by the Spirit of his mouth. And he shall be bound and shall be plunged into the abyss of everlasting fire alive with his father Satan; and all people, who do his wishes, shall perish with him forever; but the righteous ones shall inherit everlasting life with the Lord for ever and ever" (Ephraem the Syrian, *On the Last Times, the Antichrist, and the End of the World*, A.D. 373).

Ephraem believed in the imminency of the return of Christ and urged his fellow Christians to live godly lives in expectation of His return.

Actually, Ephraem the Syrian was not alone in interpreting Bible prophecy literally in his day.

He was living one generation from the era of Augustine (354-430), at which time there was a dramatic change. When Ephraem died in 373, Augustine was 19 years old.

It was in the era of Augustine that allegoricalism widely replaced the previous method of interpretation. Prior to this, it was common among Bible believers to interpret prophecy literally. They believed that Christ would return literally (and imminently), bind Satan, and establish a literal millennial kingdom on earth.

This is acknowledged by church historians.

William Newell said, "The early Church for 300 years looked for the imminent return of our Lord to reign, and they were right" (Newell, *Revelation*).

Phillip Schaaf said, "... the most striking point in the eschatology of the ante-Nicene age [prior to AD 325] is the prominent chiliasm, or millennarianism, that is the belief of a visible reign of Christ in glory on earth with the risen saints for a thousand years, before the general resurrection and judgment" (*History of the Christian Church*, 8 vols., Wm. B. Eerdmans Publishing Co., 1960, 2:614).

Henry Thiessen said, "It is clear ... that the Fathers held not only the pre-millennial view of Christ's coming, but also regarded that coming as imminent. The Lord had taught them to expect His return at any moment, and so they looked for Him to come in their day. Not only so, but they also taught His personal return as being immediately, with the exception of the Alexandrian Fathers, who also rejected other fundamental doctrines" (Thiessen, *Introductory Lectures in Systematic Theology*, p. 477).

In fact, Augustine, "the father of amillennialism," once believed in a literal millennium himself. He said, "I myself, too, once held this opinion. ... They who do believe them are called by the spiritual, Chiliasts, which we may literally reproduce by the name Millenarians" (Augustine, *City of God*, book 20, chapter 7).

The following statement by **Irenaeus** (c. 120-203) is an example of what was commonly believed among the early "church fathers," as they looked forward to Christ's return and the establishment of His kingdom:

> "The predicted blessing, therefore, belongs unquestionably to the times of the kingdom, when the righteous shall bear rule upon their rising from the dead; when also the creation, having been renovated and set free, shall fructify with an abundance of all kinds of food, from the dew of heaven, and from the fertility of the earth. ... In like manner [the Lord declared] that ... all animals feeding [only] on the productions of the earth, should [in those days] become peaceful and harmonious among each other, and be in perfect subjection to man" (Irenaeus, *Against Heresies*, The Ante-Nicene Fathers).

The church at Antioch long interpreted Bible prophecy literally. Antioch was an important church founded by Barnabas and Paul, and it is from this church that the first foreign missionaries were ordained and sent out (Acts 11:19-26; 13:1-4). It was at Antioch that the disciples of Christ were first called Christians.

Some of the preachers associated with Antioch were Lucian (died 312), Theodore (AD 350-428), Chrysostom (AD 354-407), Theodoret (AD 386-458), and Diodorus of Tarsus.

These men interpreted Bible prophecy literally and believed in a literal millennium.

In *History of Interpretation,* F.W. Farrar observed, "Diodorus of Tarsus' books were devoted to an exposition of Scripture in its literal sense, and he wrote a treatise, now unhappily lost, 'on the difference between allegory and spiritual insight'" (Farrar, pp. 213-15).

"The Antioch's school's two greatest exegetes, Theodore of Mopsuestia (AD 350-428) and John Chrysostom (AD 354-407), were 'anti-allegorical'" (Matthew Allen, "Theology Adrift: The Early Church Fathers and Their Views of Eschatology," bible.org).

Some of the early Christians after the apostles taught a form of dispensationalism. Examples can be found in the extant writings of Justin Martyr, Irenaeus, Tertullian, and Methodius. Justin Martyr (100-165) believed in four phases of history in God's plan: From Adam to Abraham, from Abraham to Moses, from Moses to Christ, and from Christ to the eternal state. Irenaeus (120-202) taught something similar, dividing the dispensations into the creation to the flood, the flood to the law, the law to the gospel, the gospel to the eternal state.

Dr. Larry Crutchfield observes that some of the early church leaders "came very close to making nearly the same divisions modern dispensationalists do" ("Rudiments of Dispensationalism in the Ante-Nicene Period," *Bibliotheca Sacra*, Oct. 1987).

The allegorical method of interpretation was invented by false teachers after the apostolic era as the apostasy was growing and spreading toward the formation of the Roman Catholic Church.

A school was established at Alexandria, Egypt, which became the headquarters for the allegorical method of interpretation. Egypt was a place where false teaching proliferated in the first centuries after Christ.

Clement, who headed the school from AD 190 to 202, corrupted the Christian faith by mixing it with the worldly philosophy and allegoricalism of Philo. He taught many false doctrines, including purgatory, and believed that most men would eventually be saved even though Jesus said only a few would be (Mt. 7:14). "Clement saw the literal meaning of Scripture as being a 'starting point' for interpretation. Although it was 'suitable for the mass of Christians,' God revealed himself to the spiritually advanced through the 'deeper meaning' of Scripture. In every passage, a deeper or additional meaning existed beyond the primary or immediate sense" (Matthew Allen, "Theology Adrift: The Early Church Fathers and Their Views of Eschatology," bible.org).

Origen (AD 185-254) was one of the chief fathers of allegoricalism. He led the school at Alexandria from AD 202 to 232. Though he endured persecution and torture for the cause of Christ under the Emperor Decius in 250, Origen was laden down with heresies. Like Clement, he mixed the truth of the Bible with pagan philosophy. He taught that celibacy was a holy state above marriage, contrary to the teaching of the apostles. He taught baptismal regeneration, purgatory, and the pre-existence of the human soul. He taught that all men, even Satan and demons, would eventually be saved. He taught that the Holy Spirit was the first creature made by God, and denied the full Godhead and eternality of Jesus. He did not believe that the Scriptures are wholly inspired by God.

Origen claimed that "the Scriptures have little use to those who understand them literally." He described the literal meaning of Scripture as "bread" and encouraged the student to go beyond this to the "wine" of allegoricalism, whereby one can become intoxicated and transported to heavenly realms. Origen's commentaries contained a wealth of fanciful interpretations, abounding in "heretical revisals of Scripture" (Frederick Nolan, *Inquiry into the Integrity of the Greek Vulgate*, p. 367).

Another father of allegoricalism was **Augustine** (AD 354-430), one of the fathers of the Roman Catholic Church. He was exalted as one of the "doctors" of Rome. Augustine invented the terrible and unbiblical doctrine of the inquisition that was used by the Catholic Church against Bible believers for more than 1,000 years. The German historian Neander observed that Augustine's teaching "contains the germ of the whole system of spiritual despotism, intolerance, and persecution, even to the court of the Inquisition." Augustine instigated persecutions against the Donatists who were striving to maintain pure biblical churches. He taught that "the sacraments," such as baptism, were the means of salvation. He taught that Mary did not commit sin. He taught the heresy of purgatory. He was one of the fathers of infant baptism, claiming that unbaptized infants are lost and calling all who rejected infant baptism "infidels" and "cursed." He exalted the authority of "the church" over that of Scripture.

"Through Augustine, Origen's allegorical hermeneutic became the backbone of medieval interpretation of the Bible" (Matthew Allen, "Theology Adrift: The Early Church Fathers and Their Views of Eschatology," bible.org).

These heresies grew and became a fundamental part of the Roman Catholic and Orthodox Churches.

When the Protestant denominations (e.g., Lutheran, Anglican, Presbyterian, Methodist) broke away from Rome, one of the errors they brought with them was the allegorical interpretation of prophecy.

The Importance of a Pre-Trib Rapture

The doctrine of the Pre-Tribulation Rapture is not a minor one. As we have seen, Jesus, Paul, James, and Peter taught that the return of Christ was imminent and was to be expected at any time (Mt. 24:44; Phi. 4:5; Jas. 5:8-9; 1 Pe. 4:7).

The early Christians lived in expectation of Christ's return and the literal fulfillment of the prophecies (1 Th. 1:9-10).

The doctrine of a Pre-Tribulation Rapture is a great motivator for purifying one's personal Christian life.

1. It encourages the believer in trials and persecutions. "Then we which are alive and remain shall be caught up together with them in the clouds, to meet the Lord in the air: and so shall we ever be with the Lord. Wherefore comfort one another with these words" (1 Th. 4:17-18).

2. It keeps the church's focus on the Great Commission (Mt. 28:18-20; Mr. 16:15; Lu. 24:44-48; Ac. 1:8). It teaches us that preaching the gospel, baptizing and discipling believers, and establishing churches as the pillar and ground of the truth is the most urgent matter. D.L. Moody had it right when he said: "I look upon this world as a wrecked vessel. God has given me a lifeboat and said to me, 'Moody, save all you can.'"

3. It motivates us to be busy in the Lord's work (1 Co. 15:58).

4. It motivates us to live obedient lives (1 Jo. 3:1-3; 1 Th. 5:4-7).

5. It motivates us to separate from evil (Tit. 2:13-14).

6. It keeps believers on the outlook for heresy and apostasy (2 Ti. 4:3-4; 1 Jo. 2:24-28).

What about the Pre-wrath Position?

The "pre-wrath" doctrine says that the Rapture occurs mid-way between Daniel's 70th Week. It is based on the view that the "church" is to be kept from God's wrath but the wrath is limited to the last half of the seven-year tribulation period, beginning when the Antichrist sets himself up as God in the Jewish temple.

I believe this position is wrong for three reasons, chiefly.

1. The first reason is the Bible's teaching about the imminency of Christ's coming, as we have already emphasized (Mt. 24:44; 44; 25:13; Mr. 13:33; Php. 4:5; 1 Th. 1:10; Jas. 5:8-9; 1 Pe. 4:7). This is a fundamental Bible teaching, but if the believer is not taken away until part way through the Tribulation, he would know the time of the Rapture precisely, almost to the day, because he would see the events unfold during the first half of Daniel's 70th week as recorded in the book of Revelation.

2. We do not accept the idea that only the last seven judgments are the wrath of God (Re. 15:1; 16:1). The wrath of God is mentioned in Revelation 6:16-17, *at the beginning* of the Tribulation. The fact is that the entire Tribulation is the wrath of God, each part growing in intensity. The seal judgments affect a fourth of the earth (Re. 6:8). The trumpet judgments affect a third of the earth (Re. 8:7-11; 9:15). The vial judgments affect the entire world (Re. 16:2, 3, 4, 8, 10, 14, 20).

3. The entire period of Daniel's 70th Week pertains to Israel and not to the church. As we have seen, the church is not seen on earth after Revelation 3. Everything described on earth in Revelation 6-18 pertains to the Gentile nations and to Israel. The "pre-wrath" position does not make a proper and consistent distinction between Israel and the church.

What about 2 Thessalonians 2?

Some use this passage as a proof text to support the position that the Rapture of church age saints occurs *after* the appearance of the Antichrist, but it teaches the opposite.

If Paul is saying in 2 Thessalonians 2 that the Rapture will occur after the revelation of the Antichrist, then he is contradicting what he taught in the first epistle to the Thessalonians.

Paul had taught the Thessalonians a lot about Bible prophecy in general and about the Rapture in particular.

Every chapter of 1 Thessalonians mentions the coming of Christ. 1 Thessalonians contains the greatest teaching on the Rapture in the Bible (1 Th. 4:13-18). Paul used used this doctrine to comfort the believers ("wherefore comfort one another with these words," 1 Th. 4:18). The Rapture would not be a comfort if it occurred after the coming of the Antichrist and the judgments described in Revelation. Paul had taught them that the coming of the Lord for them is to be expected at any time; it is imminent (1 Th. 1:10). He taught them that they were waiting on the coming of the Lord Himself, not the Antichrist. He taught them that they would not be overtaken by the destruction and darkness and wrath that will come upon the world at the day of the Lord (1 Th. 5:1-9).

Sometime after they had received the teaching of 1 Thessalonians, the saints at Thessalonica had been shaken by false teaching that the day of Christ was at hand or *already* present. In 2 Th. 2:2, "at hand" means present. The Greek word, "enistemi," is usually translated "present" (Ro. 8:38; 1 Co. 3:22; 7:26; Ga. 1:4; He. 9:9).

We believe that the solution to the apparent contradiction between what Paul taught about the Rapture in 1 Thessalonians and about the "day of Christ" in 2 Thessalonians is to understand that the "day of Christ" here refers not to the Rapture, but to "the day of the Lord" that Paul warned about in 1 Th. 5:2-9 and described as destruction and darkness and wrath. If we read 2 Th. 2:3 as follows, there are no contradictions: "Let no man deceive you by any means: for that day [the day of the Lord] shall not come, except there come a falling away first, and that man of sin be revealed, the son of perdition."

2 Thessalonians 2 was specifically written so that the believers would not be shaken in mind and troubled by the false teaching that the day of Christ had already happened. In some places, "at hand" means imminent," but here, it means present. As we have seen, the Greek word "enistemi" is

usually translated "present" (Ro. 8:38; 1 Co. 3:22; 7:26; Ga. 1:4; He. 9:9). (On the other hand, in Philippians 4:5; 1 Peter 4:7; and Revelation 1:3, "at hand" is translated from "eggus," meaning near, imminent.) The comfort is the fact that we will be gathered unto Christ before the wrath and darkness come. This is the believer's Blessed Hope. We are looking for the coming of Christ, not the coming of the Antichrist. What comfort would there be in teaching that we are waiting for the Antichrist? That would be a strange type of comfort! It would have the effect of doing the very thing that Paul was wanting to correct, that is to trouble and shake the mind.

> "A crucial question arises in verse 1 concerning the small word which Paul uses: 'concerning' (Greek 'huper'). The problem is whether he is beseeching the saints 'about' the coming of our Lord or 'by' the coming of our Lord. If the first is the meaning, then the passage seems to teach that the Rapture and the Day of the Lord are one and the same event, since the following verses clearly deal with the Day of the Lord. If the second is the meaning, then Paul is appealing to them on the basis of the prior Rapture, that they should not think they were in the Day of the Lord. The question is debatable. We agree with William Kelly when he adopts the second view: 'The comfort of the Lord's coming is employed as a motive and means for counteracting the uneasiness created by the false presentation that the day (of the Lord) was there.' We understand Paul to be saying, 'I appeal to you on the basis of the Rapture that you should not fear that you are in the Day of the Lord. The Rapture must take place first. You will be taken home to heaven at that time and will thus escape the horrors of the Day of the Lord" (*Believer's Bible Commentary*).

The "falling away" is the final apostasy that accompanies the revelation of the Antichrist. It is not merely the widespread apostasy of the end of the church age as described in 2 Timothy 2-3; it is the complete apostasy of the revelation of the religion of Revelation 17 which is associated with the rise of the Antichrist. After the Rapture, there will be no born again churches on earth, only unregenerate Christians in all of the denominations, and they will be swept up in accepting the Antichrist.

About Way of Life's eBooks

Since January 2011, Way of Life Literature books have been available in eBook format. Some are available for purchase, while others are available for free download.

The eBooks are designed and formatted to work well on a variety of applications/devices, but not all apps/devices are equal. Some allow the user to control appearance and layout of the book while some don't even show italics! For best reading pleasure, please choose your reading app carefully.

For some suggestions, see the reports "iPads, Kindles, eReaders, and Way of Life Materials," at www.wayoflife.org/database/ebook.html and "About eBooks, eReaders, and Reading Apps" at www.wayoflife.org/help/ebooks.php.

Publications for These Times

Following is a selection of the titles published by Way of Life Literature. The books are available in both print and eBook editions (PDF, Kindle, ePub). The materials can be ordered via the online catalog at the Way of Life web site -- www.wayoflife.org -- or by phone 866-295-4143.

BIBLE TIMES AND ANCIENT KINGDOMS: TREASURES FROM ARCHAEOLOGY. ISBN 978-1-58318-121-8. This is a package consisting of a book and a series of PowerPoint and Keynote (Apple) presentations which are a graphical edition of the book. The PowerPoints are packed with high quality color photos, drawings, historic recreations, and video clips. Bible Times and Ancient Kingdoms is a course on Bible geography, Bible culture, and Bible history and has a two-fold objective: to present apologetic evidence for the Bible and to give background material to help the student better understand the setting of Bible history. We cover this fascinating history from Genesis to the New Testament, dealing with the Table of the Nations in Genesis 10, the Tower of Babel, Ur of the Chaldees, Egypt, Baal worship, the Philistines, the Canaanites, David's palace, Solomon and the Queen of Sheba, Ahab and Jezebel, the fall of the northern kingdom of Israel, the Assyrian Empire, Hezekiah and his times, Nebuchadnezzar and his Babylon, the Medo-Persian Empire, Herod the Great and his temple, the Roman rule over Israel, and the Roman destruction of Jerusalem. Many of the archaeological discoveries from the past 200 years, which we relate in the course, are so fascinating and improbable that they read like a novel. It is easy to see God's hand in this field, in spite of its prevailing skepticism. The course also deals with Bible culture, such as weights and measures, plant and animal life, Caesar's coin, the widow's mite, ancient scrolls and seals, phylacteries, cosmetics, tombs, and the operation of ancient lamps, millstones, pottery wheels, and olive presses. The course begins with an overview of Israel's geography and a timeline of Bible history to give the student a framework for better understanding the material. Each section includes maps to help the student place the events in their proper location. The course is packed with important but little-known facts that illuminate Bible history and culture. The preparation for the book is extensive, the culmination of 40 years of Bible study, teaching, and research trips. In this context the author built a large personal library and collected information from major archaeological museums and locations in North America, England, Europe, Turkey, and Israel. We guarantee that the student who completes the course will read the Bible with new eyes and fresh enthusiasm. 500 pages book + DVD containing 19 PowerPoint presentations packed with more than 3,200 high quality color photos, drawings, historic recreations, and video clips.

THE FUTURE ACCORDING TO THE BIBLE. ISBN 978-1-58318-172-0. One of the many reasons why the Bible is the most amazing and exciting book on earth is its prophecies. The Bible unfolds the future in great detail, and The Future According to the Bible deals in depth with every major prophetic event, including the Rapture, the Judgment Seat of Christ, the Tribulation, the Antichrist, Gog and Magog, the Battle of Armageddon, the Two Witnesses, Christ's Return, Muslim nations in prophecy, the Judgment of the Nations, the resurrection body, the conversion of Israel, the highway of the redeemed, Christ's glorious kingdom, the Millennial Temple, the Great White Throne judgment, and the New Jerusalem. The first two chapters deal at length with the amazing prophecies that are being fulfilled today and with the church-age apostasy. Knowledge of these prophecies is essential for a proper understanding of the times and a proper Christian worldview today. The 130-page section on Christ's kingdom describes the coming world kingdom in more detail than any book we are familiar with. Every major Messianic prophecy is examined. Prophecy is a powerful witness to the Bible's divine inspiration, and it is a great motivator for holy Christian living. In this book we show that the Lord's churches are outposts of the coming kingdom. The believer's position in Christ's earthly kingdom will be determined by his service in this present world (Revelation 2:26-27; 3:21). The book is based on forty years of intense Bible study plus firsthand research in Israel, Turkey, and Europe.

BAPTIST MUSIC WARS. ISBN 978-1-58318-179-9. This book is a warning about the transformational power of Contemporary Christian Music to transport Bible-believing Baptists into the sphere of the end-time one-world "church." The author is a musician, preacher, and writer who lived the rock & roll "hippy" lifestyle before conversion and has researched this issue for 40 years. We don't believe that good Christian music stopped being written when Fanny Crosby died or that rhythm is wrong or that drums and guitars are inherently evil. We believe, rather, that Contemporary Christian Music is a powerful bridge to a very dangerous spiritual and doctrinal world. The book begins by documenting the radical change in thinking that has occurred among independent Baptists. Whereas just a few years ago the overwhelming consensus was that CCM was wrong and dangerous, the consensus now has formed around the position that CCM can be used in moderation, that it is OK to "adapt" it to a more traditional sacred sound and presentation technique. The more "conservative" contemporary worship artists such as the Gettys are considered safe and their music is sung widely in churches and included in new hymnals published by independent Baptists. As usual, the driving force behind this change is the example set by prominent leaders, churches, and schools, which we identify in this volume. The heart of the book is the section giving eight reasons for rejecting Contemporary Christian Music (it is built on the lie that music is neutral, it is worldly, it is ecumenical, it is charismatic, it is experienced-oriented, it is permeated with false christs, it is infiltrated with homosexuality, and it weakens the Biblicist stance of a church) and the section answering 39 major arguments that are used in defense of CCM. We deal with the popular argument that since we have selectively used hymns by Protestants we should also be able to selectively use those by contemporary hymn writers. There are also chapters on the history of CCM and the author's experience of living the rock & roll lifestyle before conversion and how the Lord dealt with him about music in the early months of his Christian life. The book is accompanied by a DVD containing two video presentations: *The Transformational Power of Contemporary Praise Music* and *The Foreign Spirit of Contemporary Worship Music*. 285 pages.

BELIEVER'S BIBLE DICTIONARY. This volume, the product of forty years of study, is based upon the King James Bible and is written from a dispensational, Baptist perspective. The studies are thorough, practical, devotional, and designed to be used by preachers, teachers, and homeschoolers. The *Believer's Bible Dictionary* is designed to be more affordable and transportable than the *Way of Life Encyclopedia of the Bible & Christianity*. We encourage every believer, young and old, to have his own Bible dictionary and to have it right beside his Bible as he studies, and we are convinced that this is one of the best Bible dictionaries available today. There are eight ways it can help you: **(1) It can help you understand the Bible**. The first requirement for understanding the Bible is to understand its words. **(2) It can help you understand out-of-use words and phrases from the King James Bible**, such as blood guiltiness, die the death, and superfluity of naughtiness. **(3) It can help you to do topical studies**. The student can study the full range of Bible doctrines by following the thousands of cross references from entry to entry. **(4) It can help you to study issues relating to morality and practical Christian living**, such as capital punishment, child training, cremation, and divorce. **(5) It can help you to study Old Testament types of Christ**, such as day of atonement, high priest, Melchizedek, passover, and tabernacle. **(6) It can help you to find the meaning of Bible customs and ancient culture**, such as agriculture, idolatry, military, money, music, and weights and measures. **(7) It can help you to study Bible places and geography**, such as Assyria, Babylon, Caesarea, Ephesus, and Jordan River. **(8) It can help you in preaching and teaching**. The doctrinal material in this dictionary is presented in a practical manner with outlines that can be used for teaching and preaching, in the pulpit, Sunday Schools, Bible Colleges and Institutes, home schools, family devotions, prisons and jails, nursing homes, etc. Missionary author Jack Moorman calls the dictionary "excellent" and says, "The entries show a 'distilled spirituality.'" Second edition May 2015. 385 pages.

THE DISCIPLING CHURCH: THE CHURCH THAT WILL STAND UNTIL JESUS COMES. New for March 2017. This church planting manual aims to establish churches on a solid biblical foundation of a regenerate church membership, one mind in doctrine and practice, serious discipleship, thorough-going discipline, and a large vision for world evangelism. We examine the New Testament pattern of a discipling church, and we trace the history of Baptist churches over the past 200 years to document the apostasy away from the biblical pattern to a mixed multitude philosophy. We also document the history of "sinner's prayer" evangelism which has affected the reality of a regenerate church membership. The book deals with biblical salvation with evidence, care in receiving church members, the church's essential first love for Christ, the right kind of church leaders, the right kind of preaching, training church members to be Bible students, the many facets of church discipline, building strong families, youth ministry, training preachers, charity, reproof, educating the church for spiritual protection, maintaining standards for workers, the church's prayer life, the church's separation, spiritual revival, the church's music, and many other things. The last chapter documents some of the cultural factors that have weakened churches over the past 100 years, including the theological liberalism, public school system, materialism and working mothers, the rock & roll pop culture, pop psychology, the feminist movement, New Evangelicalism, television, and the Internet. There is also a list of recommended materials for a discipling church. 550 pages.

THE EFFECTUAL BIBLE STUDENT. This is a 12-hour series of video presentations plus an accompanying textbook containing a detailed outline to the course. It is our goal and passion to help God's people, including teenagers, become effectual Bible students. The course, which is the product of 40 years of Bible study and teaching, has life-changing potential. It has four major sections: (1) The spiritual requirements for effectual Bible study, (2) tips for daily Bible study, (3) principles of Bible interpretation, and (4) how to use Bible study tools. It also deals with using Bible study software on a computer, a tablet, or a smartphone. It is a package consisting of the videos of the course and the textbook with review questions for testing. The course notes can be used as a standalone tool by teachers to teach church classes and home schooling programs or can be used for self-study. The package can be purchased as a set of 6 DVDs and a textbook, or it can be downloaded for free from www.wayoflife.org.

KEEPING THE KIDS: HOW TO KEEP THE CHILDREN FROM FALLING PREY TO THE WORLD. ISBN 978-1-58318-115-7. This book aims to help parents and churches raise children to be disciples of Jesus Christ and to avoid the pitfalls of the world, the flesh, and the devil. The book is a collaborative effort. It contains testimonies from hundreds of individuals who provided feedback to our questionnaires on this subject, as well as powerful ideas gleaned from interviews with pastors, missionaries, and church people who have raised godly children. The book is packed with practical suggestions and deals with many issues: Conversion, the husband-wife relationship, the necessity of permeating the home with Christian love, mothers as keepers at home, the father's role as the spiritual head of the home, child discipline, separation from the pop culture, discipleship of youth, the grandparents' role, effectual prayer and fasting. Chapter titles include the following: "Conversion," "The Home: Consistent Christian Living and the Husband-Wife Relationship," "Child Discipline," "The Church," "Unplugging from the Pop Culture," "Discipleship," "The Grandparents," "Grace and the Power of Prayer." 531 pages.

THE MOBILE PHONE AND THE CHRISTIAN HOME AND CHURCH. ISBN 978-1-58318-198-0. Many Christian homes and churches are losing a frightful percentage of their young people to the world. This practical and far-reaching youth discipleship course deals with the parent's part, the church's part, and the youth's part in discipling young people. It covers salvation, child discipline, the Christian home environment that produces disciples, reaching the child's heart, Bible study techniques, how to protect young people from dangers associated with the Internet and smartphones, how to use apologetics, and many other things. The section on building a wall of protection deals with such things as having a basic home phone that teens can use under parental oversight, using filters and accountability software, controlling passwords and apps, the power of pornography, the dangers of *Facebook* and video games, avoiding conversation with members of the opposite sex, and monitoring the young person's attitude. The course explains how the church and the home can work together in youth discipleship. It describes the characteristic of a church that produces youth disciples, such as having qualified leaders, officers, and teachers, maintaining biblical standards for workers, being careful about salvation, being uncompromising about separation from the world, building godly homes, discipline, prayer, and vision. It deals with how to train young people to be effective Bible students and how to involve them in the church's ministry. Finally, the course deals with eleven biblical principles of spiritual protection that young people must build into their own lives. These are living to please the Lord, living by the law of the Spirit, practicing humility, pursuing Christian growth, pursuing edification and ministry, pursuing honesty, practicing vigilance and separation, pursuing pure speech, redeeming the time, pursuing temperance, and obeying and honoring one's parents. 200 pages. The *Mobile Phone* youth discipleship course can be downloaded as a free eBook from www.wayoflife.org.

MUSIC FOR GOOD OR EVIL. This video series, which is packed with photos, video and audio clips, has eight segments. **I. Biblical Principles of Good Christian Music. II. Why We Reject Contemporary Christian Music.** It is worldly, addictive, ecumenical, charismatic, shallow and man-centered, opposed to preaching, experience-oriented, and it weakens the strong biblicist stance of a church. **III. The Sound of Contemporary Christian Music.** In this section we give the believer simple tools that he can use to discern the difference between sensual and sacred music. We deal with syncopated dance styles, sensual vocal styles, relativistic styles, and overly soft styles that do not fit the message. **IV. The Transformational Power of Contemporary Worship Music.** We show why CCM is able to transform a "traditional" Bible-believing church into a New Evangelical contemporary one. Its transformational power resides in its enticing philosophy of "liberty" and in its sensual, addictive music. We use video and audio to illustrate the sound of contemporary worship. **V. Southern Gospel.** We deal with the history of Southern Gospel, its character, its influence, and the role of the Gaithers in its renaissance. This section is packed with audio, video, and photos. **VI. Marks of Good Song Leading.** There is a great need for proper training of song leaders today, and in this segment we deal with the following eight principles: Leadership, preparation, edification, spirituality, spiritual discernment, wisdom in song selection, diversity. One thing we emphasize is the need to sing worship songs that turn the people's focus directly to God. We give dozens of examples of worship songs that are found in standard hymnals used by Bible-believing churches, but typically these are not sung properly as "unto God." **VII. Questions Answered on Contemporary Christian Music.** We answer 15 of the most common questions on this subject, such as the following: Is rhythm wrong? Isn't this issue just a matter of different taste? Isn't the sincerity of the musicians the important thing? Isn't some CCM acceptable? Didn't Luther and the Wesleys use tavern music? What is the difference between using contemporary worship hymns and using old Protestant hymns? **VIII. The Foreign Spirit of Contemporary Worship Music.** This presentation documents the frightful spiritual compromise, heresy, and apostasy that permeate the field of contemporary praise. Through extensive documentation, it proves that contemporary worship music is controlled by "another spirit" (2 Co. 11:4). It is the spirit of charismaticism, the spirit of the "latter rain," the spirit of Roman Catholicism and the one-world "church," the spirit of the world that is condemned by 1 John 2:16, the spirit of homosexuality, and the spirit of the false god of *The Shack*. The presentation looks carefully at the origin of contemporary worship in the Jesus Movement of the 1970s, examining the lives and testimonies of some of the most influential people. 5 DVDs.

ONE YEAR DISCIPLESHIP COURSE, ISBN 978-1-58318-117-1. This powerful course features 52 lessons in Christian living. It can be broken into sections and used as a new converts' course, an advanced discipleship course, a Sunday School series, a Home Schooling or Bible Institute course, or for preaching outlines. The lessons are thorough, meaty, and very practical. There is an extensive memory verse program built into the course, and each lesson features carefully designed review questions. Following are some of the lesson titles (some subjects feature multiple lessons): Repentance, Faith, The Gospel, Baptism, Eternal Security, Position and Practice, The Law and the New Testament Christian, Christian Growth and Victory, Prayer, The Armor of God, The Church, The Bible, The Bible's Proof, Daily Bible Study, Key Principles of Bible Interpretation, Foundational Bible Words, Knowing God's Will, Making Wise Decisions, Christ's Great Commission, Suffering in the Christian Life, The Judgment Seat of

Christ, Separation - Moral, Separation - Doctrinal, Tests of Entertainment, Fasting, Miracles, A Testing Mindset, Tongues Speaking, The Rapture, How to Be Wise with Your Money, The Believer and Drinking, Abortion, Evolution, Dressing for the Lord. 8.5X11, coated cover, spiral-bound. 221 pages.

THE PENTECOSTAL-CHARISMATIC MOVEMENTS: THE HISTORY AND THE ERROR. ISBN 1-58318-099-0. The 5th edition of this book, November 2014, is significantly enlarged and revised throughout. The Pentecostal-charismatic movement is one of the major building blocks of the end-time, one-world "church," and young people in particular need to be informed and forewarned. The author was led to Christ by a Pentecostal in 1973 and has researched the movement ever since. He has built a large library on the subject, interviewed influential Pentecostals and charismatics, and attended churches and conferences with media credentials in many parts of the world. The book deals with the history of Pentecostalism beginning at the turn of the 20th century, the Latter Rain Covenant, major Pentecostal healing evangelists, the Sharon Schools and the New Order of the Latter Rain, Manifest Sons of God, the charismatic movement, the Word-Faith movement, the Roman Catholic Charismatic Renewal, the Pentecostal prophets, the Third Wave, and recent Pentecostal and charismatic scandals. The book deals extensively with the theological errors of the Pentecostal-charismatic movements (exalting experience over Scripture, emphasis on the miraculous, the continuation of Messianic and apostolic miracles and sign gifts, the baptism of the Holy Spirit, the baptism of fire, tongues speaking, physical healing guaranteed in the atonement, spirit slaying, spirit drunkenness, visions of Jesus, trips to heaven, women preachers, and ecumenism). The final section of the book answers the question: "Why are people deluded by Pentecostal-Charismatic error?" David and Tami Lee, former Pentecostals, after reviewing a section of the book said: "Very well done! We pray God will use it to open the eyes of many and to help keep many of His children out of such deception." A former charismatic said, "The book is excellent and I have no doubt whatever that the Lord is going to use it in a mighty way. Amen!!" 487 pages.

A PORTRAIT OF CHRIST: THE TABERNACLE, THE PRIESTHOOD, AND THE OFFERINGS. ISBN 978-1-58318-178-2. This book is an extensive study on the Old Testament tabernacle and its priestly system, which has been called "God's masterpiece of typology." Whereas the record of the creation of the universe takes up two chapters of the Bible and the fall of man takes up one chapter, the tabernacle, with its priesthood and offerings, takes up 50 chapters. It is obvious that God has many important lessons for us in this portion of His Word. Speaking personally, nothing has helped me better understand the Triune God and the salvation that He has purchased for man, and I believe that I can guarantee that the reader will be taken to new heights in his understanding of these things. Everything about the tabernacle points to Jesus Christ: the design, the materials, the colors, the court walls and pillars, the door into the court, the sacrificial altar, the laver, the tabernacle tent itself with its boards and curtains and silver sockets, the tabernacle gate, and veil before the holy of holies, the candlestick, the table of shewbread, the incense altar, the ark of the covenant, the high priest, and the offerings. All is Christ. The tabernacle system offers brilliant, unforgettable lessons on Christ's person, offices and work: His eternal Sonship, His sinless manhood, His anointing, His atonement, His resurrection glory, His work as the life and sustainer and light of creation, His eternal high priesthood and intercession, and His kingdom. In addition to the studies on every aspect of the tabernacle, *A Portrait of Christ* features studies on the high priest, the Levitical priests, the five offerings of Leviticus, the day of atonement, the ransom money, the red heifer, the cherubims, strange fire, the golden calf, leprosy, the Nazarite vow, the pillar of cloud and pillar of fire, and the transportation of the tabernacle through the wilderness. The tabernacle is very practical in its teaching, as it also depicts believer priests carrying Christ through this world (1 Pe. 2:5, 9). Like the Israelites in the wilderness, believers today are on a pilgrimage through a foreign land on the way to our eternal home (1 Pe. 2:11). Don Jasmin, editor of the *Fundamentalist Digest* says, "This new book on the Tabernacle constitutes the 21st-century classic treatise of this rich theme." 420 pages.

SEEING THE NON-EXISTENT: EVOLUTION'S MYTHS AND HOAXES. ISBN 1-58318-002-8. This book is designed both as a stand alone title as well as a companion to the apologetics course *AN UNSHAKEABLE FAITH*. The contents are as follows: Canals on Mars, Charles Darwin and His Granddaddy, Thomas Huxley: Darwin's Bulldog, Ernst Haeckel: Darwin's German Apostle, Icons of Evolution, Icons of Creation, The Ape-men, Predictions, Questions for Evolutionists, Darwinian Gods, Darwin's Social Influence. The **ICONS OF EVOLUTION** that we refute include mutations, the fossil record, homology, the peppered moth, Darwin's finches, the fruit fly, vestigial organs, the horse series, the embryo chart, the Miller experiment, Archaeopteryx, bacterial resistance, the big bang, and billions of years. The **ICONS OF CREATION** that we examine include the monarch butterfly, the trilobite, the living cell, the human eye, the human brain, the human hand, blood clotting, the bird's flight feathers, bird migration, bird song, harmony and symbiosis, sexual reproduction, living technology, the dragonfly, the bee, and the bat. The section on **APE-MEN** deals with Cro-Magnon, Neanderthal, Java Man, Piltdown Man, Nebraska Man, Peking Man, Lucy, Ardi, Ida, among others. The section on **PREDICTIONS** considers 29 predictions made by Biblical creationism, such as the universe will behave according to established laws, the universe will be logical, and there will be a vast unbridgeable gulf between man and the animal kingdom. **DARWINIAN GODS** takes a look at inventions that evolutionists have devised to avoid divine Creation, such as panspermia and aliens, self-organization, and the multiverse. 608 pages.

SOWING AND REAPING: A COURSE IN EVANGELISM. ISBN 978-1-58318-169-0. This course is unique in several ways. *It is unique in its approach.* While it is practical and down-to-earth, it does not present a formulaic approach to soul winning, recognizing that individuals have to be dealt with as individuals. The course does not include any sort of psychological manipulation techniques. It does not neglect repentance in soul winning, carefully explaining the biblical definition of repentance and the place of repentance in personal evangelism. It explains how to use the law of God to plow the soil of the human heart so that the gospel can find good ground. *The course is unique in its* *objective.* The objective of biblical soul winning is not to get people to "pray a sinner's prayer"; the objective is to see people soundly converted to Christ. This course trains the soul winner to pursue genuine conversions as opposed to mere "decisions." *The course is also unique in its breadth.* It covers a wide variety of situations, including how to deal with Hindus and with skeptics and how to use apologetics or evidences in evangelism. There is a memory course consisting of 111 select verses and links to a large number of resources that can be used in evangelism, many of them free. The course is suitable for teens and adults and for use in Sunday School, Youth Ministries, Preaching, and private study. OUTLINE: The Message of Evangelism, Repentance and Evangelism, God's Law and Evangelism, The Reason for Evangelism, The Authority for Evangelism, The Power for Evangelism, The Attitude in Evangelism, The Technique of Evangelism, Using Tracts in Evangelism, Dealing with Skeptics. 104 pages, 8x11, spiral bound.

THINGS HARD TO BE UNDERSTOOD: A HANDBOOK OF BIBLICAL DIFFICULTIES. ISBN 1-58318-002-8. This volume deals with a variety of biblical difficulties. Find the answer to the seeming contradictions in the Bible. Meet the challenge of false teachers who misuse biblical passages to prove their doctrine. Find out the meaning of difficult passages that are oftentimes overlooked in the Bible commentaries. Be confirmed in your confidence in the inerrancy and perfection of the Scriptures and be able to refute the skeptics. Learn the meaning of difficult expressions such as "the unpardonable sin." A major objective of this volume is to protect God's people from the false teachers that abound in these last days. For example, we examine verses misused by Seventh-day Adventists, Roman Catholics, Pentecostals, and others to support their heresies. We deal with things such as the blasphemy against the Holy Spirit, cremation, head coverings, did Jesus die on Friday, God's repentance, healing in the atonement, losing one's salvation, sinless perfectionism, soul sleep, and the Trinity. Jerry Huffman, editor of *Calvary Contender*, testified: "You don't have to agree with everything to greatly benefit from this helpful book." In researching and writing this book, the author consulted roughly 500 volumes, old and new, that deal with biblical difficulties and the various other subjects addressed in *Things Hard to Be Understood.* This one volume, therefore, represents the essence of a sizable library. Sixth edition Feb. 2014, enlarged and completely revised, 441 pages.

AN UNSHAKEABLE FAITH: A CHRISTIAN APOLOGETICS COURSE. ISBN 978-1-58318-119-5. The course is built upon nearly 40 years of serious Bible study and 30 years of apologetics writing. Research was done in the author's personal 6,000-volume library plus in major museums and other locations in America, England, Europe, Australia, Asia, and the Middle East. The package consists of an apologetics course entitled *AN UNSHAKEABLE FAITH* (both print and eBook editions) plus an extensive series of Powerpoint/Keynote presentations. (Keynote is the Apple version of Powerpoint.) The 1,800 PowerPoint slides deal with archaeology, evolution/creation science, and the prophecies pertaining to Israel's history. The material in the 360-page course is extensive, and the teacher can decide whether to use all of it or to select only some portion of it for his particular class and situation. After each section there are review questions to help the students focus on the most important points. The course can be used for private study as well as for a classroom setting. Sections include The Bible's Nature, The Bible's Proof, The Dead Sea Scrolls, The Bible's Difficulties, Historical Evidence for Jesus, Evidence for Christ's Resurrection, Archaeological Treasures Confirming the Bible, A History of Evolution, Icons of Evolution, Icons of Creation, Noah's Ark and the Global Flood.

WAY OF LIFE ENCYCLOPEDIA OF THE BIBLE & CHRISTIANITY. ISBN 1-58318-005-2. This hardcover Bible encyclopedia contains 640 pages (8.5x11) of information, over 6,000 entries, and over 7,000 cross-references. Twenty-five years of research went into this one-of-a-kind reference tool. It is a complete dictionary of biblical terminology and features many other areas of research not often covered in such volumes, including Bible Versions, Denominations, Cults, Christian Movements, Typology, the Church, Social issues and practical Christian living, Bible Prophecy, and Old English Terminology. It does not correct the Authorized Version of the Bible, nor does it undermine the fundamental Baptist's doctrines and practices as many study tools do. The 5th edition (October 2008) contains new entries, extensive additions to existing entries, and a complete rewriting of the major articles. Many preachers have told us that apart from *Strong's Concordance*, the *Way of Life Bible Encyclopedia* is their favorite study tool. A missionary told us that if he could save only one study book out of his library, it would be our Bible encyclopedia. An evangelist in South Dakota wrote: "If I were going to the mission field and could carry only three books, they would be the Strong's concordance, a hymnal, and the *Way of Life Bible Encyclopedia*." Missionary author Jack Moorman says: "The encyclopedia is excellent. The entries show a 'distilled spirituality.'" 5th edition, 640 pages. A computer edition of the encyclopedia is available as a standalone eBook for PDF, Kindle, and ePub. It is also available as a module for *Swordseacher*.

Way of Life Literature
P.O. Box 610368, Port Huron, MI 48061
866-295-4143, fbns@wayoflife.org
www.wayoflife.org
